BEST·OF·FRIENDS,
FESTIVE OCCASIONS

COOKBOOK

For People On-The-Go

BY

DARLENE GLANTZ SKEES

ILLUSTRATED BY

JODI JENSEN
&
ANN BISHO

Darlene Glantz Skees
804 47th Street South
Great Falls, MT 59405
(406) 727-2811

Published by Darlene Glantz Skees—Rembrandt Productions, MT.

To order additional copies please write to the above address. Inquiries welcome concerning fundraising projects.

1st Printing

ISBN 0-9619158-2-X

LIBRARY OF CONGRESS CATALOG NUMBER:
93-92726

Written, published and
printed in Montana
Copyright© 1993 by Darlene Glantz Skees

Other Volumes in Print
Best of Friends, Etc., Vol. I
ISBN 0-9619158-0-3

Best of Friends, Too
ISBN 0-9619158-1-1
L.I.C. 90-91505

REVIEWER'S VIEWS

Fellow "Best of Friends" fans—

Darlene has again diligently burned the midnight oil to perfect a very special collection of festive and holiday cuisine for people on-the-go! Of course, every day is a "festival" and Darlene's many special and unique recipes make our efforts in the kitchen festive rather than drudgery. We know you can hardly wait to delve into the pages of Volume 3—"Best of Friends, Festive Occasions"—so ENJOY!

MEET WATERCOLORIST, JODI JENSEN

JODI JENSEN IS THE CREATOR OF "GARDEN NIBBLERS" A WATERCOLOR WHICH EMBELLISHES THE COVER OF VOLUME 3 "BEST OF FRIENDS, FESTIVE OCCASIONS" COOKBOOK. JODI HAS ALSO "LOANED" HER MANY BUNNIES TO ROMP THROUGH "FESTIVE OCCASIONS" WHERE THEY PLAYFULLY POSE WHILE SMELLING THE FLOWERS AND NIBBLING THE CARROTS.

Watercolorist Jodi Jensen is best known for her beautiful florals, adorable bunnies and creative children's illustrations. She began drawing at the age of three. In high school she started developing her painting skills, using oil as her medium. It wasn't until her university studies that she started painting with watercolors, which is her favorite medium in which to express herself. Jodi studied art at Brigham Young University, which included a semester of art history in Vienna, Austria, as well as intensive watercolor and figure drawing classes in Hawaii. These unique experiences have blended together to play an important role in the development of her style. Jodi lives in northern California along with her husband Dave, three children, four Holland and Mini Lop bunnies, three cats, fish and a bird.

Look for Jodi's work in every state and in many foreign markets.

MEET THE CREATOR OF HOLLY DAY

Ann Patterson Bishop was born in Denver, Colorado and attended Colorado State University, the University of Rome and Red Rocks College. She was employed as a visual information specialist (illustrator) for the Bureau of Land Management for 15 years. She now devotes full time to artistic endeavors, including establishing her own business, "Pig Ridge Products," which manufactures "software" kitchen items, i.e. aprons, potholders, bread bakery covers, etc. She created the logo for the Montana Wildlife Federation and has to her credit several awards for her art work. "Holly Day," an adorable Montana Angora, is Ann's contribution to the holiday chapter of "Best of Friends—Festive Occasions."

HOLLY DAY'S FAVORITE SOFT SUGAR COOKIES
(aka Grandma's Soft Sugar Cookies)

2 cups flour	1 egg yolk
1/2 teaspoon soda	1/2 cup sour milk
1 teaspoon salt	1/2 teaspoon vanilla
1/2 cup shortening	1 egg white (stiffly beaten)
1 cup granulated sugar	

PREHEAT OVEN: 375 degrees F.

In a medium bowl mix together flour, soda and salt. Set aside. In a large mixer bowl, cream shortening, sugar, and egg yolk until fluffy. Add flour mixture alternately with the milk and vanilla. Fold in egg white. Drop batter by rounded tablespoon 3 inches apart on a greased cookie sheet. Flatten to 1/2-inch thickness with cookie press or other utensil such as measuring cup or drinking glass, etc. Sprinkle with sugar. Bake 20 minutes or until lightly browned.

BONUS: Grease the bottom of glass or other utensil before pressing cookie dough. Add 1 teaspoon lemon juice or vinegar to sour the milk.

TABLE OF CONTENTS

ACKNOWLEDGEMENTS

Gary Anderson
Pam Anderson
Alice Beltrone
Linda Boeshart
Jo Jo
Miriam Bramlette
Marilyn Brown
Francis X. Clinch
Tootie Clintworth Myhre
Janece "Gooch" Connor
Garnet Dahmer
Joyce Dearborn
Susan Dell
Mary Dykstra
Sally Eaton
Anna May Erickson
Pam Erickson
Pat Erickson
Joyce Faechner
Jeanne Fleming
Erma Franscioni
Marilyn Frazier
Donna Gill
Clara Glantz
Marianne Granlie
Betty Grant
Helen Grove
Lori Harper
Delsea Hassell
Sue Hastings
Gladys Herman
Stella Jakel
Greta Peterson Johnson

Marilyn Kelley
Janet Knox
Sharon Knudson
Jane Larson
Kathleen Lorenz
Sherry Maar
Mary Mason
Peggy Matteucci
Connie McCabe
Dorothy "Dottie" McGee
June Meiners
Judy Neil
Norbys of Aberdeen
Diane Ocon
Helen Pluhar
Carmen Poulsen
Joyce Reid
Darlene Schmid
Bev Sherman
Bertie Sigvardt
Bertha "B" Skees
Darlene Skees
Pam Skiba
Josy Slaymaker
Bobbie Smedsrud
Pat Strand
Patty Surak
Jim Thares
Janet Tiffany
Pam VanCamp
Nona Jane VanDyck
Leslie Vaskey
Marlene Williams

Special thanks to Susan & Lori who spent many hours proofing and indexing.

FOREWORD

Writing Volume 3 "Best of Friends, Festive Occasions" was a real labor of love, but without friends and family it could not have been accomplished. Thanks to all who contributed recipes, tested and enjoyed eating them, and special thanks to my proofreaders who spent many hours dotting the i's and crossing the t's.

ENJOY!

Darlene

P.S. 🍎 denotes the end of a recipe.

KITCHEN MEASUREMENTS

For best results when cooking it is important to use the right measurements.
- Use GLASS MEASURING CUPS to measure any kind of Liquid.
- Use DRY MEASURING CUPS to measure flour, sugar, shortening, etc.
- Use MEASURING SPOONS to measure such ingredients as salt, spices, etc.
- For less than 1/4 cup use standard measuring spoons.
- The term "dash" indicates less than 1/8 teaspoon.

LIQUID MEASUREMENTS
1 cup = 8 fluid ounces
2 cups = 16 fluid ounces
4 cups = 32 fluid ounces
2 cups = 1 pint
2 pints = 1 quart
1 quart = 4 cups
4 quarts = 1 gallon

DRY MEASUREMENTS
3 teaspoons = 1 tablespoon
4 tablespoons = 1/4 cup
16 tablespoons = 1 cup
2 tablespoons = 1 ounce
4 ounces = 1/4 pound
16 ounces = 1 pound
1 pound = 454 grams

ONE-POUND EQUIVALENTS
2 cups butter
4 cups all purpose flour
2 cups granulated sugar
3-1/2 cups powdered sugar, packed
2-1/4 cups brown sugar, packed

METRIC MEASUREMENTS
1 teaspoon = 5 milliliters
1 tablespoon = 15 milliliters
1 cup = 240 milliliters
1 ounce = 28 grams
1 pound = 454 grams

PERSPICACIOUS HINTS
...Darlene

Again, I am nearing the "end of the road" in completion of Volume 3–"Best of Friends, Festive Occasions." It has been a tedious and sometimes–"why am I writing yet another cookbook" situation, but when the holidays rolled around, I knew there had to be just one more cookbook for my "best friends."

Volume 3 is actually two books-in-one. A special holiday section separates the book in two parts. I know you will have great fun - some of the special features include:

...Several recipes just for the "kids" in your life. Whether you are a mother, grandmother, aunt or just a best friend–I know you will find someone special to join in the festival of creating cookies and candies for Christmas and other holidays throughout the year.

...Menu-type entries that give hints on what to serve when!

...Again–substitutions are welcome where feasible. If you are on a special diet, add to or detract from the ingredients. Many of my friends find this no problem at all with "Best of Friends" recipes.

...And–of course–the nutmeg is still alive and healthy. I'm sure you all must have that nutmeg grinder tucked away in a special drawer by now! It continues to be my favorite spice.

...All recipes have been tested for altitude of 3200 feet. You may have to adjust for higher altitude baking.

...Again–if the computer gremlin has stolen the baking temperature, borrow from a similar recipe. However, 350 degrees F. remains the norm for most baking.

Lastly–some of the recipes may seem "long." The format of Volume 3 is somewhat different than the first two volumes. However, this was done to make reading and using the recipe easier for the user.

Don't be "threatened" by a 2-page recipe. I promise easy-to-follow - and ingredient availability country-wide.

My motto remains "Easy and Elegant For People On-The-Go."

Hoppy cooking!

P.S. I'm still working as a paralegal!

POTABLES:

POTABLES
Index

REFRESHING TEQUILA PUNCH

A "must" for the punch-bunch. A refreshing tag-along to those spicy little appeteasers and southwestern cuisine. Also, this punch rates an "A" on its own merits.

2 46-ounce cans
   unsweetened grapefruit
   juice, chilled
4 cups tequila

1 cup lemon juice
2 12-ounce cans or bottles
   of ginger ale, chilled
Lots of cracked or cubed ice

Stir together the grapefruit juice, tequila and lemon juice. Chill. To serve, pour half of this mixture over ice in a very large punch bowl. Slowly pour in half of the ginger ale and stir gently just to mix.

Repeat with the remaining punch as needed.

YIELD: 24 to 30 6-ounce servings

PLANTER'S PUNCH

Planter's Punch was made popular in the Caribbean basically because of the rum, pineapple juice and other juices employed in its derivation. With or without the rum, it is indeed a refreshing beverage.

1/2 cup granulated sugar
1 cup boiling water
2 cups dark rum
1-1/2 cups unsweetened
   pineapple juice
1-1/2 cups orange juice

1/2 cup lemon juice or
   lime juice
1 tablespoon grenadine
   syrup

Ice cubes

FOR SYRUP: Combine the sugar and water; stir until sugar dissolves. Chill.

In pitcher combine the syrup, rum, pineapple juice, orange juice, lemon juice or lime juice and grenadine.

Serve over ice cubes and garnish with orange and lime slices if desired.

BONUS: The punch can be made and served from a punch bowl or served individually in tall glasses. Use plenty of ice.

YIELD: 6 10-ounce servings

SPARKLING CITRUS SANGRIA

Just one of many "portable" potables to enjoy at a barbecue or family reunion. This citrus sangria is not typical but may become so after you have enjoyed its distinctive flavor.

1 bottle (750 ml) dry red wine	1/2 cup fresh lime juice
2 cups fresh squeezed orange juice	1/2 cup fresh lemon juice
	1/4 cup granulated sugar
	Sparkling water (club soda)

In a large pitcher, combine the wine, orange juice, lime juice and lemon juice. Stir in sugar. Cover and chill.

Just before serving stir in 2 cups sparkling water.
Garnish with orange slices.

BONUS: Recipe doubles nicely

YIELD: 8 cups

JUICY FRUIT COOLER

An interesting amalgamation of flavors that turns out to be refreshing any time of the year, but exceptionally tasty in the summertime.

2 6-1/2-ounce bottles sparkling mineral water, chilled
1 12-ounce can peach nectar, chilled

1/2 cup unsweetened orange juice, chilled
1/4 cup unsweetened grapefruit juice, chilled
2 tablespoons lemon juice, chilled

In a glass pitcher, combine all ingredients, mix well. Pour over ice in tall glasses. Serve immediately.

BONUS: Recipe can be doubled to serve more guests.

YIELD: 4 servings

BLUSHING STRAWBERRY DAIQUIRIS

Beautiful to look at, fun to create, and delicious. Strawberry daiquiris are indubitably drinkable.

6 ounces limeade
  concentrate
10 ounces frozen
  strawberries in syrup

3/4 cup light rum

Crushed ice

Add half of the first three ingredients in electric blender. Blending well, add enough crushed ice to make the mixture slushy. Empty blender and repeat procedure with the remaining half of the ingredients.

The first three ingredients for the daiquiris may be frozen up to two weeks. When ready to use, thaw slightly, place in blender and add crushed ice to make mixture slushy.

BONUS: To add something novel to these already-scrumptious daiquiris, add a small banana to the first three ingredients and proceed with the concoction.

Garnish with a slice of banana or fresh strawberry when available.

YIELD: Serves 8

ITALIAN SODA

Genuinely refreshing, Italian sodas are generally available throughout the United States and most readily obtainable at a sidewalk coffee/soda bar. I prepare them in my kitchen and you can do the same in yours.

PER SERVING:

1-1/2 ounces flavored soda
    syrup
8 ounces plain club soda

1 tablespoon light cream
    (half and half)
Ice

Fill a tall glass with cubed ice. Add flavored soda syrup and fill remainder of glass with plain club soda. Stir the mixture and top with light cream. Lightly stir again. Taste and enjoy!

BONUS: Flavored syrups can be found in individual servings at most kitchenware stores or stores that carry specialty food mixes, etc. Bigger containers can be purchased in some "upbeat super markets." I make my own concentrated syrups such as the Raspberry Shrub recipe from "Best of Friends, Too!" My friends like the raspberry, huckleberry, boysenberry and cherry flavors the best. I "borrowed" some of my wild plum pancake syrup for a taste test and it was spectacular. If you can't find the flavorings in your area, ask your favorite grocer if he can locate them. (Promise him a sample if he finds an outlet for you).

YIELD: 1 serving

HAWAIIAN PARTY PUNCH

A friendly standby, many variations of this effortless punch exist. Particularly great for those birthday party celebrations.

1 12-ounce can of each of the following concentrates:

Frozen lime, orange and lemon concentrates
1 12-ounce can Hawaiian Punch® Seven-Up or Gingerale

Dilute the concentrates lightly. Add Hawaiian punch and gingerale or seven-up to taste. Chill.

Serve in tall glasses over ice with a wedge of fresh pineapple impaled on rim of glass for garnish.

BONUS: For a fancier garnish, freeze ice cubes with a fresh mint leaf inside. Mix plain and mint cubes in each glass. Serve with fancy colored straws to complete the "pretty-as-a-picture" treat.

YIELD: Recipe can be doubled to serve a big bunch of "kids."

❦

—NOTES—

APPETEASERS:

APPETEASERS
Index

ROQUEFORT GRAPES—
A SOPHISTICATED BEGINNING

For those of us who possess a passion for roquefort, this elegant appeteaser is indeed the greatest beginning to any special repast. What else can I say??

PREHEAT OVEN: 275 degrees F.

1 10-ounce package almonds, pecans or walnuts toasted

1 8-ounce package Lite cream cheese

1/8 pound roquefort cheese

2 tablespoons whipping cream

1 pound seedless grapes— red or green—washed and dried

To toast nuts, spread them on a baking sheet and bake just until lightly toasted. (Almonds should be a light golden brown color; pecans and walnuts should smell toasted but not burned.)

Chop toasted nuts coarsely in food processor or by hand. Spread chopped nuts on a platter.

In the bowl of an electric mixer, mix the cream cheese, roquefort cheese and cream, beating until smooth.

Recipe Continues...

ROQUEFORT GRAPES—
A SOPHISTICATED BEGINNING

Continued...

Drop the clean, dry grapes into the cheese mixture and gently stir by hand to coat them. Roll the cheese-coated grapes in the toasted nuts and place on a waxed-paper lined tray. Chill finished grapes before serving.

Serve on a silver tray alongside a bunch of "plain" grapes.
Alert your guests that the grapes are indeed for eating. They look so beautiful that your guests may think that they are just for decoration.

BONUS: The original recipe calls for the nuts to be chopped coarsely. I have better luck using finely chopped nuts. I suggest doing whatever is easiest for you, or do some of each.

YIELD: 50 grapes

APRICOT CHICKEN WINGS

This recipe for speedy chicken wings comes from a "Best of Friends" fan who lives in Litchfield, Minnesota. The wings can be made ahead of time and held over for those latecomer guests.

3 - 4 pounds chicken wings

1 small jar apricot jam

1 8-ounce bottle Russian
   dressing

1/2 **package dry onion
soup mix**

Mix the jam, Russian dressing and onion soup mix together and pour over the chicken wings. (It is easiest if you microwave the jam first.)

BAKE at 350 degrees F. for 2 hours. If your guests arc late, turn temperature down and continue baking.

BONUS: Marlene says it is usually ok to leave wings in oven for 2 to 3 hours for those very late guests.

SPECIFICALLY CEVICHE

A classic fish favorite from Mexico, Spain and South America (it is pronounced Suh-VEESH) and most often served as an appeteaser in North America. I enjoyed this unusual treat without knowing what it was and then searched for a recipe, which took some time to capture. It can be somewhat likened to our tomato salsa only Ceviche is created with fish. It is a keeper.

1 pound fresh or frozen haddock fillets or other fish fillets
1 cup fresh lime juice or lemon juice—I prefer lime
1 small onion
2 or 3 jalapeño peppers
1/4 cup extra virgin olive oil
3/4 teaspoon salt
1/4 teaspoon dried oregano leaves
1/8 teaspoon pepper
2 medium tomatoes

Cut fish into 1/2-inch cubes. Place the cubed fish fillets in a "non-metal" bowl and cover with the lime or lemon juice. Cover and chill at least 4 hours or overnight until fish is opaque. Stir occasionally during this process.

Thinly slice the onion and separate into rings. Rinse, seed and cut jalapeño peppers into strips. Add the onion, peppers, olive oil, salt, oregano and pepper to the fish. Toss gently, cover and chill.

Recipe Continues...

SPECIFICALLY CEVICHE

Continued...

Before serving peel, seed and chop the tomatoes; toss with the chilled fish mixture. Spoon into a serving bowl.

BONUS: I originally experienced Ceviche as an appeteaser served with crackers. It would do very nicely with a Mexican buffet. Don't hesitate trying it because the fish is raw. Actually the acid in the lime juice "cooks" the fish.

YIELD: Serves 10 to 12

WALNUT SAMPLERS

A basic cocktail "nibbler," also can be dispersed over a "greens" salad that is lacking originality. Take a little gift bag when you travel to a friend's home for dinner.

PREHEAT OVEN: 450 degrees F.

3/4 cup walnut halves
1 teaspoon Canola oil
   (vegetable oil)
2 teaspoons granulated
   sugar

1/4 teaspoon salt
1/8 teaspoon ground cumin
   (don't leave out)
Generous pinch of red
   pepper flakes

In a small mixing bowl, place walnuts, add the Canola oil and stir well to mix. Add remaining ingredients and toss to coat. Place the nuts in an 8" x 8" cake pan and bake until lightly browned. Stir occasionally. This process should take about 7 to 8 minutes.

BONUS: Tastiest served warm but also can be handed out at room temperature.

YIELD: Depending on size of walnuts a single recipe will yield about 3/4 cup. However, I suggest you double or triple the recipe for a generous supply.

CHILE-FLAKE PARMESAN TOASTETTES

A real south-of-the-border appeteaser, this yummy treat can be enjoyed any place in the world!

PREHEAT OVEN: 400 degrees F.

1 cup "lite" mayonnaise
1 cup shredded fresh
   parmesan cheese

6 green onions, chopped
6 English muffins
Dried red pepper flakes

Combine the mayonnaise, parmesan and onions. Spread on English muffin halves—do not be penurious!

Place on cookie sheet, bake at 400 degrees F. for 5-10 minutes or until lightly toasted.

For serving, cut each muffin half into 4 wedges. Be sure to have extra on hand because they will disappear in a flash.

BONUS: If red pepper flakes are too spicy, sprinkle some dehydrated bacon bits on top instead. Chopped artichoke hearts are enjoyable too!

YIELD: 6 MUFFINS—48 wedges

B L T STUFFED CHERRY TOMATOES

If you fancy BLT sandwiches, I know you will devour these tasty mini versions. Super at a cocktail party or as a buffet side dish. Any way you serve them will be met with satisfying enjoyment.

1/2 **pound lean bacon, broiled crisp and crumbled**
1/4 **cup chopped green onion (I use a small bunch)**

2 **tablespoons chopped fresh parsley—or dried**
2 **tablespoons grated Parmesan cheese—don't leave out**
1/2 **cup low fat mayonnaise**
24 **cherry tomatoes**

Mix all ingredients, except tomatoes. Scoop out inside of whole cherry tomatoes and spoon in the stuffing. Chill and serve on lettuce-lined platter. Parsley is for garnish.

BONUS: A small "melon-baller" works great for scooping out inside of tomatoes or a tiny demitasse spoon works even better. (Somehow one of these showed up in my silverware drawer).

You can use more bacon if desired.

YIELD: 24 stuffed tomatoes

30

SHRIMP DILL PARTY RYES

These delicate party ryes meet with greatest approval served at a bridal shower or high tea.

8-ounce package low fat
  cream cheese
1 cup low fat mayonnaise
1 package Good Seasons
  Farm Style Dressing Mix

1 8-ounce can cocktail
  shrimp—rinsed and drained
Party Rye slices
Dill weed

Cucumber slices

Combine softened cream cheese, mayonnaise and dressing mix of your choice. Fold in the shrimp. Spread on rye slices and top with a thin slice of cucumber. Dust sparingly with dill weed.

BONUS: Spread can be made ahead of time and refrigerated. Hidden Valley Dressing Mix may be substituted.

MINI ZUCCHINI PIZZAS

I'll bet you have never heard of zucchini pizza. The prolific zucchini strikes again and I don't mean "out." This fantastic appeteaser is worth repeating so plan on using that profusion in your garden soon.

PREHEAT BROILER: Place rack 5 inches from heat source.

Large zucchini
Salt
1 tablespoon pizza sauce—
   homemade or purchased
1 teaspoon chopped black
   olives

3 green onions minced
1 tablespoon grated
   Monterey Jack cheese or
   any other white cheese of
   your choice

Cut zucchini in 1/4-inch thick slices.
On each slice of zucchini place above ingredients in the order given.

Place pizzas on baking sheets and broil until cheese is melted and bubbling. This will take about 4 to 5 minutes—zucchini should be crispy.

Remove from oven and serve warm.

BONUS: Prepare pizzas ahead of time and broil after your guests have arrived or as soon as the "kids" have have washed their hands before dinner.

YIELD: Depends on size of zucchini

BAKED STUFFED ZUCCHINI BITES

These zucchini bites are not in the least "stuffy." They make a very friendly appearance on a buffet table or as a summertime fill-in at the picnic table.

PREHEAT OVEN: 350 degrees F.

6 small (6" to 8") zucchini
3/4 cup tomato chopped fine
1/4 cup finely chopped
   onion
1-1/2 cups grated sharp
   cheddar cheese

1 egg
Salt and pepper to taste

Crisp bacon or bacon bits

Slice zucchini lengthwise. Using a spoon, scrape the pulp from the zucchini halves. Grate the zucchini pulp. (Marianne uses her salad shooter.)

Mix the grated pulp and all remaining ingredients together except for the bacon bits. Cook in skillet about 2 to 3 minutes or just until mixture firms slightly.

Place cooked mixture in zucchini "boats" and sprinkle generously with crisp bacon. Place on baking sheet, cover with foil and bake for 10 minutes; remove foil and bake another 10 minutes.

Slice into bite size servings.

BONUS: Serve warm from the oven.

ASPARAGUS & SHRIMP ROUNDS

Curry powder adds a bit of the exotic to these atypical before-dinner toast rounds.

PREHEAT OVEN: 350 degrees F.

1/2 cup low fat mayonnaise
1/3 cup chopped water
   chestnuts
1/4 teaspoon curry powder
1 10-ounce can asparagus
   tips (drained) or fresh
   cooked

1 4-1/4-ounce can tiny
   cocktail shrimp, rinsed
   and drained
40 to 45 melba toast rounds
Toasted sesame seed
   (optional)

In a small mixing bowl, mix together the mayonnaise, water chestnuts and curry powder. Carefully stir in the asparagus and shrimp. Spread about a rounded teaspoonful of the mixture on each melba toast. At this point, sprinkle on the toasted sesame seed if desired.

Place rounds on ungreased baking pan or cookie sheet. Bake for 10 to 12 minutes or until entirely heated. Best served warm.

BONUS: These tasty little rounds can be prepared at least 2 hours before serving. Cover and keep refrigerated until baking time.

YIELD: 40 - 45

CHILE RELLENO CHEESE SQUARES

Delicious, hasty and hot! These spicy appeteaser squares are a super addition to a Mexican dinner or accompanied by a frosty Margarita.

PREHEAT OVEN: 300 degrees F.

1 4-ounce can chopped green chiles or jalapeños drained

3/4 pound Monterey Jack or sharp cheddar cheese, grated

4 large eggs, beaten

Grease an 8" x 8" square baking pan. Spread green chilies or jalapeños over bottom of pan. Sprinkle the cheese over the chilies. Pour eggs over cheese and bake 1 hour at 300 degrees F., until center tests firm.

Cool and cut into 25 squares.

BONUS: If prepared ahead of time, the squares can be frozen. Place on cookie sheet and flash freeze. When frozen, put in freezer bags and keep frozen until needed. Bake frozen squares for 15 minutes at 350 degrees in conventional oven or heat by microwaving.

This recipe can be baked in a pie plate and served in wedges for a brunch entree.

YIELD: 25 squares

PEPPERED CHEESE COOKIES

Unobtrusive appeteaser cookies spiked with red pepper will draw rave reviews from all who partake. I guarantee a big hit with the "in" crowd.

8 ounces sharp cheddar
   cheese, grated
2 sticks (1 cup) margarine
   softened

2 cups all-purpose flour
2 cups Rice Krispies® cereal
1/2 teaspoon red pepper
1/2 teaspoon salt

Cream the margarine and cheese. Add flour, red pepper, salt and cereal. Mix well.

Roll into small balls and press flat with a fork. Cookies should be about 1-inch in diameter.

BAKE at 350 degrees F. for 15 minutes.

BONUS: Absolutely yummy appeteaser cookies. Make splendid house gifts carried to your hostess in a miniature gift bag. Cookies can be frozen.

YIELD: 5 dozen

PIROSHKI (QUICK 'N EASY)

There are many variations of this fantastic Polish appeteaser. This recipe takes a short-cut or two, but suffice it to say, the following method is a time-saver and good tasting to boot!

PREHEAT OVEN: 400 degrees F.

1 package refrigerated
  ready-made pie crusts

2 minced large onions
2 tablespoons butter or
  margarine
3/4 pound extra lean
  ground beef

1 teaspoon dried dill weed
1/2 teaspoon salt
1/8 teaspoon pepper
2 hard-cooked eggs,
  chopped

Prepare pie crusts according to directions on package.
Roll out pie crusts so they are a bit thinner than they come prepackaged. Cut into circles using a 2-inch round cookie cutter or biscuit cutter.

Prepare filling by lightly sautéeing onions in the melted butter. Add the ground meat and cook, stirring until lightly browned.

Cool the above mixture before adding the remaining ingredients, making certain to blend thoroughly.

Recipe Continues...

PIROSHKI (QUICK 'N EASY)
Continued...

Place a rounded teaspoon of the mixture in center of one-half of each circle, fold over to the top edge, covering the meat mixture. Using a fork that has been dipped in cold water, crimp and seal the edges.

Place piroshki on greased cookie sheets and bake for 25 - 30 minutes or until golden.

Serve hot.

BONUS: You can substitute 1 package or 2 sticks pie crust mix. You can also leave out the hard-cooked eggs and substitute 1/4 pound mushrooms, finely chopped and sautéed with the onion. Then you can freeze the appeteasers. I do not suggest that you freeze the piroshki with the chopped egg in them.

YIELD: 6 servings

SUSAN'S ROTEL® DIP

This extra-easy appeteaser is almost too rudimentary to print out. It is one recipe that you can remember without taking notes and is always reliable.

1 2-pound package Velveeta® cheese	1 pound lean ground beef 1 can Rotel, drained

Brown ground beef; melt cheese in microwave on medium. In a large bowl mix the browned ground beef, the melted cheese and the can of Rotel®.

Serve with your favorite chips.

BONUS: Rotel® is a mixture of green chilies and tomatoes found in the Mexican food section of your favorite grocery store. Also, if you want a nacho-type dip, you can leave out the ground beef.

If you don't do microwave, melt the cheese in the fry pan after you have browned the beef, but be sure to drain any grease that may have been left over from the beef.

❧

—NOTES—

BREADS:

BREADS
Index

FRIENDLY COWBOY BREAD
aka FRIENDSHIP BREAD

This friendly bread is really like a snack cracker bread. The idea is to serve it amongst friends who then break off a piece from the whole. It is delicious with beer or served with soups. In other words, it is friendly to just about any "festive occasion."

PREHEAT OVEN: 350 degrees F.

1 cup warm water
1 tablespoon dry yeast
1 teaspoon granulated sugar
1/4 cup Canola or other
   vegetable oil

1/2 teaspoon salt
3 cups bread flour
   (all purpose is okay)

In a large bread bowl, mix together warm water, yeast and sugar. Add the oil, salt and 2 cups of the flour. Stir until flour is incorporated; add the remaining 1 cup of flour, mix and knead 3 - 5 minutes until dough is smooth. Dough will be a little sticky to handle.

Cover and let rise 1 hour. Punch down, divide into four pieces and let rest 10 minutes.

Recipe Continues...

43

FRIENDLY COWBOY BREAD
aka FRIENDSHIP BREAD
Continued...

Roll dough to cookie sheet size. Place on a greased cookie sheet and spread with fingers until very thin (as for pizza dough). Prick all over with a fork and bake at 350 degrees F. for 15 minutes.

Brush immediately with melted butter when taken from the oven. Dehydrated Parmesan or American cheddar cheese sprinkled over bread is a must.

Let bread cool and break into serving pieces to share with friends.

BONUS: Store in tin container to keep crisp.
I like to use pizza pans to bake the bread. Cookie sheets are fine but if you do have a pizza pan, try it.

YIELD: 4 bread rounds

GRANDMA'S GREBELS
(aka German Fry bread)

This fry bread was enjoyed by all of our family when I was still living at home as a child. It was typically used as a bread to be served with soups and at our house it was served with chili. The fry bread is best warm.

5 cups all purpose flour
4 eggs
1/3 cup granulated sugar
1 pint sour cream

1 teaspoon baking soda
1 teaspoon baking powder
1 teaspoon salt
1 teaspoon melted butter

In a large mixing bowl place the flour. In a small bowl, beat the eggs, add the sugar, baking soda, baking powder, sour cream and salt. Add the wet mixture into the flour mixture and combine well. Add the melted butter.

Add a little more flour if needed to make a soft dough.

Cover dough and refrigerate overnight or for at least 6 hours.

Recipe Continues...

GRANDMA'S GREBELS
(aka German Fry bread)
Continued...

To make Grebels—roll out a small portion of the dough into a rectangle about 1/4-inch thick; cut dough into 3-inch squares, cut a couple of slits in the middle of the square and deep fat fry for a few minutes. Watch carefully so the Grebels do not burn or get overly browned. They should look somewhat like a "fritter." Remove Grebel from fryer and roll in granulated sugar while still warm.

Repeat with remaining dough.

BONUS: My mother likes to make the dough just before she goes to bed, but you can make it early in the day and have it ready for lunch. I like it best on a wintry day.

❦

POPPYSEED QUICK BREAD

Poppyseed goodies are in great demand. This quick bread is "quick" to put together. Have some in your freezer for those festive days that get out of hand.

BREAD:
PREHEAT OVEN: 300 degrees F.

1 cup butter
2 cups granulated sugar
4 eggs
1/2 teaspoon salt
1/2 teaspoon baking soda
3 cups all-purpose flour

1-1/2 tablespoons poppyseed
1 cup low fat buttermilk
Grated rind of 1 lemon
   (chop finely)
1 cup finely chopped
   pecans

LEMON GLAZE:
Juice of 2 lemons or 1/4 cup
   lemon juice

1 cup powdered sugar

FOR BREAD:
Cream the butter and sugar on high speed with your mixer. Add eggs one at a time, mixing well.

In another bowl, combine salt, soda, poppyseed and flour; add this to the creamed butter and sugar alternately with the buttermilk.

Recipe Continues...

POPPYSEED QUICK BREAD
Continued...

Stir in the grated lemon rind and chopped pecans.
Grease and flour one 9" x 5" loaf pan or two 7" x 3" pans. Line
bottoms with parchment paper or waxed paper. Spoon the batter
into pans and bake at 300 degrees for 1 hour 20 minutes or until
bread tests done with a toothpick.

Let bread cool in pans for at least 5 minutes. Punch holes in bread
and drizzle glaze over top. Cool before slicing.

BONUS: I like to add 1/8th teaspoon freshly ground nutmeg and a
teaspoon of vanilla for extra flavor.

QUICK BREAD TIPS:
Fill pans at least two-thirds full to allow for batter to rise.

If using raisins, dates or other dried fruits, add a small amount of
the recipe flour to the fruits so they won't "glob" up in the batter.

If you are baking at a high altitude, it is always wise to decrease
baking powder and soda by one-fourth.

Most quick breads are best if held overnight—this gives them time
to "capture" the flavors and also to make it easier to slice. I like to
use my electric knife for slicing breads—it keeps the bread from
crumbling.

CHEESE SPREAD FOR BREAD

Originally this congenial cheese spread was made with butter. Now, it is concocted with margarine. However, it still brings back many great memories of eating and dancing at a restaurant called "Red Lion" here in Great Falls. This tasty bread was always served with their soup of the house "Chicken Bisque."

1 pound margarine	1 teaspoon Worchestershire
1/2 pound grated sharp	sauce
cheddar cheese	1/4 teaspoon garlic powder
1/4 pound grated Romano	1 tablespoon horseradish
cheese	1/2 teaspoon paprika

Ingredients should be at room temperature. Combine all ingredients in a mixer bowl and slowly whip until fluffy. The cheese spread will keep in refrigerator for two weeks.

Spread cheese spread on french bread, sour dough or English muffins. Place bread on a cookie sheet and broil taking care to not overdo it.

SOUPS, SALADS, ETC.:

SOUPS, SALADS, ETC.
Index

KATHLEEN'S BLACK-EYED PEA, ETC. SOUP

A great soup that creates a complete dinner with the addition of your favorite bread or crackers and, a sumptuous chocolate dessert, of course. This soup is definitely not boring and I like to serve it at pre-game football parties.

1 cup dried navy beans
1/4 cup barley

8 cups chicken broth
4 medium onions chopped
2 large cloves garlic, crushed
2 bay leaves

1/2 teaspoon thyme
1/2 teaspoon pepper
1-1/2 teaspoons olive oil
1 pound bulk lean ground sausage formed into 1-inch balls
1/2 pound chopped broccoli
1/2 ring of Polish or Kielbasa sausage sliced

Place black-eyed peas and beans in large heavy stock pot; add water to cover by one-inch. Bring to boil, simmer 2 minutes; remove from heat, cover and let stand for one hour. Drain and return beans etc. to stock pot. Add barley at this point.

Pour in the chicken broth and bring to boil over medium heat. Add the onions, garlic, bay leaves, thyme and pepper. Return to boil, reduce heat and simmer 30 minutes or until beans are tender.

Recipe Continues...

KATHLEEN'S BLACK-EYED PEA, ETC. SOUP

Continued...

Meanwhile, in large skillet, heat 1/2 teaspoon olive oil, add the sausage balls and cook through for about 10 minutes. You can accomplish this while the beans are on "hold." Drain on paper towels.

Add Kielbasa which has been cut in slices—then in halves—and cook to remove the fat—place on paper towels.

When beans are tender add the broccoli and simmer for 15 minutes. Stir in remaining 1 teaspoon olive oil; add sausage balls and Kielbasa. Add salt if desired and heat through. Let stand 15 minutes before serving.

BONUS: The recipe may appear complicated but Kay and I can tell you that it goes together easily and quickly. Just get all of the ingredients out of the cupboards and start adding to the soup pot. Also, we like to make the soup a day ahead of serving so that it has a chance to "season." ENJOY!

YIELD: Serves many hungry football fans

CARMEN'S BLACK BEAN SOUP

Black beans have recently become readily available in our neck of the woods. I prefer the turtle beans because they are shiny black and are a little larger than most black beans. You will find Carmen's rendition of Black Bean Soup very pleasant.

1 pound dry black turtle beans
1 pound lean ham hocks
1 tablespoon vegetable oil
1 cup chopped carrots
1 cup chopped celery
2 cups chopped onion
2 tablespoons minced garlic—optional
2 teaspoons pimiento (optional)
1/2 teaspoon red pepper flakes or chili powder

2 14-ounce cans chicken broth (low sodium)
4 cups water or clear vegetable broth
1/4 teaspoon thyme
1 16-ounce can chopped tomatoes
1-1/2 teaspoons salt or to taste
1/4 teaspoon black pepper

Lemon slices for garnish

Soak beans overnight. In hot oil cook the onions, carrots and celery; cook until golden. Add garlic and other seasonings. Stir in the broths and beans; add ham hock, bring to boil and simmer for 30 minutes. Add the tomatoes and simmer another 2 hours or until beans are soft

Recipe Continues...

55

CARMEN'S BLACK BEAN SOUP
Continued...

and cooked. Remove ham hock and mash beans with a potato masher. Shred any "useable" ham from the hocks and add to the soup.

Serve with lemon slices.

BONUS: Adjust the seasoning to your liking.

YIELD: 6-8 servings

❧

CAESAR'S SALAD RENEWED

This Caesar's salad uses an egg white instead of a "coddled" egg, but I personally find that you can omit the white and still possess a magnificent Caesar. The added plus is Gary's recipe for home-made Caesar croutons.

2 ounces anchovies
  (2/3 tube)
8 tablespoons extra-virgin
  olive oil
2 pinches dry mustard
1/2 lemon—juice only
1 large head romaine lettuce

2 large cloves garlic
2 to 4 tablespoons red wine
  vinegar

10 drops Worcestershire
  sauce
1 egg white
1/2 cup grated Parmesan
  cheese—fresh is best

Gary's Home-made
  Croutons

Mix anchovy paste and minced garlic cloves together. Blend olive oil, vinegar, mustard and Worcestershire sauce together. Add anchovy/garlic paste to the oil mixture and whisk until well blended.

Before serving, add lemon juice and egg white and blend well. The Parmesan cheese should be added at this time.

Recipe Continues...

CAESAR'S SALAD RENEWED
Continued...

If using a wooden salad bowl, rub with crushed garlic then toss romaine lettuce, croutons and dressing. Garnish with additional Parmesan cheese and croutons. If using glass or other-type salad bowl, omit rubbing with garlic.

The secret to this recipe is Gary's home-made croutons.

GARY's CROUTONS:
Crush 2 - 4 large cloves of garlic and combine with 1 cup of extra-virgin olive oil. LET THIS MIXTURE MARINATE OVERNIGHT OR AT LEAST 6 HOURS. Strain before using.

Chop day-old bread (French, sourdough, Italian) and place on a cookie sheet. Pour strained olive oil and garlic mixture over the bread chunks and broil in oven until just crispy and lightly browned.

BONUS: If you are allergic to garlic it can be omitted, but the true success of this Caesar salad is the generous application of fresh garlic cloves.

NICE RICE

A "nice" side dish of white and wild rice as an accompaniment to a stir-fry entree, goulash, etc.

PREHEAT OVEN: 350 degrees F.

1/4 cup (4 oz.) butter or
   margarine
1/4 cup chopped green
   onion
2-1/2 cups chicken broth
   (home made or
   commercial low fat)

1 cup white rice
2 tablespoons wild rice
   (optional)
1/4 cup minced fresh parsley
1/2 cup sunflower seeds

Melt butter or margarine in medium skillet over medium heat. Add the onion and sauté until slightly softened.

Transfer onion to a 2-quart baking dish. Stir in remaining ingredients except the sunflower seeds.

Cover tightly and bake until broth has been absorbed—about 45 minutes.

Remove from oven, add sunflower seeds and mix with fork.

BONUS: This dish could be put together earlier in the day. Add the broth just before baking.

YIELD: 6 servings

SAUCED BROCCOLI

A "sassy" bowl of broccoli to be served with a luncheon entreé or a Sunday afternoon buffet for friends. The green of this vegetable means good health and good taste.

1 bunch fresh broccoli
1/3 cup vinegar
1/2 cup light salad oil or
   Canola oil

1 tablespoon dried dill weed
1/2 cup granulated sugar
Salt and pepper

Wash broccoli, remove most of stem and cut into pieces. Mix together vinegar, oil, dill, sugar, salt and pepper. Pour over broccoli and toss to coat. Marinate at least 6 hours, stirring once or twice. Drain and serve in a clear cut glass bowl.

BONUS: Double recipe for serving a large group

CROWD PLEASER CABBAGE

What a crowd pleaser this cabbage dish is....next to the "Scalloped Cabbage" in "Best of Friends, Etc.", this one takes the cake. Men in particular cherish the taste. On top of that, there's nothing complicated about this recipe. Be a "crowd pleaser" today. The cabbage is just "ripe" for the taking.

1 medium head of cabbage, shredded
1 small onion, chopped
1 green or red bell pepper, chopped
4 slices lean bacon
1/4 teaspoon Tabasco® Sauce
1 tablespoon sugar
1 teaspoon seasoning salt such as Alpine Touch or Accent

Fry the bacon, drain on paper toweling. Leave the bacon grease in skillet and add the onion and bell pepper. Sauté until just tender.

Add the shredded cabbage, tabasco sauce, seasoning salt and bacon. Cover pan and cook on medium heat just until cabbage is "wilted."

BONUS: You best make a double batch!

YIELD: Depending on size of cabbage

61

GLADYS' BEANS

The legumes are coming, the legumes are coming! Bring your bean bag. Of course, if you don't want to feast solely on beans, bring your plate and we'll fill it with a winsome array of leguminous delights.

1 can green lima beans
1 can red kidney beans

1 can pork and beams
2 cans white buttered beans

I use the medium sized cans of beans which vary a bit in weight but average anywhere from 10 ounces to 15 ounces.
Drain all except the pork and beans. Place all beans in large bean pot or dutch oven. Hold aside.

8 slices of lean bacon, fried
  and crumbled
3 small onions, chopped
1/2 teaspoon garlic powder
1 teaspoon salt

1 teaspoon prepared
  mustard
1/2 cup brown sugar
1/2 cup vinegar (I use Best
  of Friends raspberry
  vinegar)

Recipe Continues...

GLADYS' BEANS
Continued...

Fry and crumble the bacon. Leaving grease and bacon in pan add 3 chopped small onions, garlic powder, salt, mustard and brown sugar. Add vinegar and simmer this mixture for 20 minutes and then add to the beans and cook for 1 hour at 300 degrees F.

BONUS: These beans get better and better as days roll by. They are like a required subject but a lot more palatable. You have my personal guarantee that these beans cannot be outdone.

YIELD: 8 to 10 servings

BLACK TURTLE BEANS AND RICE

Donna sent this unusually good tasting black bean recipe to "Best of Friends" cookbooks with the comment "I did my beans in an oven and added the rice to cook up the liquid in the beans." She grades it A+. I agree with her comments and recognize it as a good healthy dish.

2 cups (1 pound) dried
   black beans
7 cups cold water
1/2 teaspoon salt
1/2 teaspoon pepper
1/2 teaspoon cumin

1 bay leaf
2 teaspoons red wine
   vinegar
2 cups low-sodium chicken
   broth
1 cup long-grain rice

Pick over the beans for stones. Soak the beans in water overnight, or use the quick-soak method: Put the beans in a large pot with a lid. Add enough water to cover the beans by several inches. Bring to a boil and boil for 2 minutes. Cover the pot, remove from the heat and let the beans stand for 1 hour.

Drain the beans. Put them in a large pot with the water and seasonings (except the vinegar). Bring to a boil, then turn back to very slow boil. Cook, uncovered until the beans are tender and most of the liquid has evaporated, about 50 minutes.

Recipe Continues...

BLACK TURTLE BEANS AND RICE
Continued...

Meanwhile, bring the broth to a boil, add the rice and reduce the heat to low. Simmer covered for 20 minutes or until done.

Stir the vinegar into the beans. Serve the beans over scoops of rice or combine the rice and beans.

BONUS: If you like your beans with more "kick" double the seasonings. Also, I like to use black turtle beans.

YIELD: Serves up to 10

❦

MASHED POTATO PATTIES

I remember my mother making a big batch of mashed potatoes for Sunday dinner and then saving leftovers for Monday's mashed potato patties.

2 quarts cold mashed potatoes	2 tablespoons dried onion flakes
2-3 eggs (enough to hold the potato mixture together)	Salt and pepper to taste
3/4 cup corn flake crumbs	1 teaspoon seasoning salt such as Alpine Touch or Accent

Cut 10 or 12 6-inch squares of waxed paper and lay the squares out on a counter.

Mix the potato mixture with your hands and shape into patties. Place each patty on a waxed paper square. Stack 3 or 4 patties together and place in a plastic bag or other plastic container and freeze.

After thawing, fry in butter or margarine about 5 to 8 minutes on each side.

GRANDMA'S FRENCH POTATO CASSEROLE

June's grandmother came from France and brought with her this delectable potato casserole. This is the dish you want to serve with a prime rib roast or a barbecued turkey.

2 cups mashed potatoes
2 cups creamed cottage cheese
Beat 1 egg and add 2 tablespoons grated onion
1 teaspoon salt

1/4 teaspoon pepper
2 tablespoons flour

1 tablespoon butter
1/4 cup grated cheese (your choice)

Blend all ingredients together and put into buttered 1-1/2 quart baking dish. Dot with 1 tablespoon butter and sprinkle 1/4 cup grated cheese on top.

BAKE AT 350 DEGREES F. for 1 hour.

BONUS: I prefer fresh parmesan cheese on top of the potatoes but cheddar is nice. The recipe doubles nicely for a crowd.

❧

MIXED VEGETABLE CASSEROLE

3 10-ounce packages frozen
  mixed vegetables
1-1/2 cups shredded sharp
  cheddar cheese
1 cup chopped celery
1 cup chopped onion
1 cup low fat mayonnaise or
  salad dressing

1/4 teaspoon pepper
1-1/2 cups crushed rich
  round crackers (about 38
  crackers)
1/4 cup butter or margarine
  softened

Cook vegetables according to package directions; drain. Combine with cheese, celery, onion, mayonnaise and pepper. Turn mixture into a 13" x 9" x 2" baking dish.

Combine crackers and margarine. Sprinkle over vegetable mixture. Bake uncovered in a 350 degree F. oven for 20 to 25 minutes or until heated through.

BONUS: Can be made early in the day. If you do so, cover with plastic wrap and save the cracker mixture until just before putting vegetables into the oven.

YIELD: 10 - 12 servings

ONIONS AND BLUE CHEESE

The combination of Walla Walla or Vidalia onions and blue cheese is admirable indeed. This side dish goes together slick as a whistle and without fail. We enjoy it with barbecued steaks but the onions and blue cheese mingle well with any entreé and fill in splendidly on a buffet table.

2 large sweet white onions
   (3 cups onions sliced
   thinly and separated into
   rings)

1/3 cup crumbled blue
   cheese
   (about 1-1/2 ounces)
1/4 cup Canola or other
   vegetable oil

1-1/2 tablespoons lemon
   juice
1/2 teaspoon salt
1/4 teaspoon granulated
   sugar
Freshly ground black
   pepper—a dash
   Dash paprika

Optional: A "squirt" of
   Cheese Italian Dressing

Place onion rings in medium bowl and pour the blue cheese mixture over all—mix to coat onions and chill for several hours. Serve in your nicest glass serving dish.

BONUS: The "squirt" of Cheese Italian dressing is optional, but I like the additional flavor it lends to the onions and blue cheese. The dressing is available at most grocery stores.

YIELD: Serves 8 - 10 nicely as a condiment

❧

BELGIAN TOMATO SALAD

If you are a gardener, this salad is "right up your alley."
For those of us who do not have ready access to nice big ripe
tomatoes and onions will just have to sojourn to the nearest
farmers market or vegetable stand.

1 large white onion	1 tablespoon basil
4 large ripe tomatoes	1 tablespoon dill weed
Salt	1 teaspoon celery seed
Sugar	
Pepper	1/4 cup French dressing
1 tablespoon chives	bottled or homemade

Slice the onion and separate into rings. Place on a flat platter round
or square. Slice the tomatoes one-half inch thick and layer over the
onion rings.

Dust lightly with salt and granulated sugar. Sprinkle pepper over
all (freshly ground is nicest). Mix the chives, basil and dill together
and sprinkle over all. Sprinkle with 1 teaspoon celery seed as a
"topper."

Pour the French dressing evenly over top of the tomato/seasoning
mixture and cover with foil. Hold in refrigerator for at least one hour
before serving.

BONUS: If you have Walla or Vidalia onions available in your
area—choose them. Otherwise any sweet white onion is okay.

YIELD: 8 servings

TRIPLE FRUIT COMBO

Exceptional light and easy this medley of fruit goes together easily and can tag along with any festive occasion. A family picnic would welcome this nicely.

DRESSING:
1 8-1/4 ounce can crushed pineapple chilled and drained
1/2 cup low-fat buttermilk
1 envelope vanilla instant breakfast mix
1 teaspoon lemon juice
Several drops almond extract

SALAD:
1 16-ounce can peach slices, chilled and drained
1 16-ounce can pear halves, chilled, drained and sliced
1 16-ounce can pitted light sweet cherries, chilled and drained (Queen Anne cherries are my choice).

For the dressing combine in a medium bowl the drained pineapple, buttermilk, dry vanilla breakfast mix, lemon juice and almond extract; set aside.

In an elegant glass bowl, combine the chilled and drained peaches pears and cherries; pour the dressing over all and toss kindly to coat.

BONUS: I like to garnish the salad with chopped macadamia or pecans.

YIELD: 8 healthy servings

–NOTES–

ENTREÉS:

ENTREÉS
Index

ALABAMA CHICKEN

A savory chicken dish such as Alabama Chicken is just what the doctor ordered. Peggy brings to the "Best of Friends" library a "sure-fire" entree that will be enjoyed by all who seize upon its guaranteed goodness.

2 pounds chicken breasts cooked and cut into chunks. (Reserve liquid.)

SAUTÉ:

1 stick (1/4 pound) margarine
1 cup chopped onions
1 cup chopped celery
1 cup chopped green bell pepper

ADD:

1 cup sliced stuffed olives
1/2 cup sliced ripe olives
1/2 pound Velveeta® cheese— cut in cubes
1 large can sliced mushrooms
1 10-3/4-ounce can cream of mushroom soup

COOK:

4-1/2 ounces green noodles in the reserved chicken broth and drain.

Mix all ingredients together and place in a 9" x 13" buttered baking pan.

Recipe Continues...

ALABAMA CHICKEN

Continued...

BAKE: 300 degrees F. for 45 minutes

BONUS: Alabama Chicken freezes very nicely. I prepare two smaller casseroles and put one in the freezer for one of those TGIF weekends.

I used 1/2 cup red bell pepper and 1/2 cup yellow bell pepper in place of 1 cup chopped green bell pepper.

YIELD: Serves 6 - 8 depending on size of appetites

LINGUINE, BASIL & BRIE

These three ingredients fuse to create a most splendid pasta experience. Those who partake will most assuredly appreciate your perspicacious choice.

4 large ripe tomatoes (peeled and seeded), cut into 1/2 inch cubes
1 pound Brie cheese (rind removed) torn into irregular pieces
1 cup fresh basil cleaned and cut into strips (or 3 tablespoons dried)
3 cloves garlic, peeled and finely minced

1 cup plus 1 tablespoon extra-virgin olive oil
1/2 teaspoon salt
1/2 teaspoon freshly ground pepper
1-1/2 pounds linguine

Freshly grated Parmesan cheese

At least 2 hours before serving combine the tomatoes, brie, basil, garlic, 1 cup olive oil, 1/2 teaspoon salt and the pepper in a large serving bowl. Cover and set aside at room temperature.

Bring 6 quarts water to boil in a large pot. Add 1 tablespoon olive oil and 1 teaspoon salt. Add linguine and boil until tender but firm—about 8 to 10 minutes.

Recipe Continues...

LINGUINE, BASIL & BRIE
Continued...

Drain pasta and immediately toss with the tomato sauce mixture. Serve at once with Parmesan and freshly ground pepper.

BONUS: Susan likes to add chicken or shrimp to make this side dish a glorious main course.

YIELD: 4 - 6 servings

GRETA'S PERFECT BEEF & PASTA CASSEROLE

Perfected for a high school class reunion the summer of '93, I begged for this recipe for "Best of Friends Festive Occasions." Although it was not my class reunion, I enjoyed the friendship of many in this particular class from Billings Senior High. It is only fitting that this extra-special dish be shared with best friends everywhere.

2-1/2 pounds lean ground beef
1/4 teaspoon garlic powder (optional)
2 tablespoons vegetable oil
3/4 cup chopped onion
1-1/4 cups chopped green bell pepper
Salt and pepper to taste

1 15-ounce can tomato sauce
1 6-ounce can tomato sauce

1 12-ounce package large noodles, cooked
Reserve one cup of noodles for garnish

1 8-ounce package light cream cheese
1 pint low fat small curd creamed cottage cheese
1 pint light sour cream

Red, green and yellow bell pepper rings for garnish
1/2 cup melted butter

In large electric fry pan or other large frying pan sauté the chopped onion and chopped bell pepper in 2 tablespoons vegetable oil. Add the ground beef and cook until light brown. Add the garlic powder, salt and pepper to taste.

Recipe Continues...

79

GRETA'S PERFECT BEEF & PASTA CASSEROLE
Continued...

Add to the meat mixture the 2 cans of tomato sauce and simmer for 15 minutes. Hold aside.

Cook the noodles, drain and hold aside in cold water. Remember to save out 1 cup of the noodles for garnish.

Blend the three cheeses together until well mixed.

Grease a 2-1/2 quart casserole or two smaller pans.

Layer one-half of the cooked noodles on bottom of pan.
Spread all of the cheese mixture over top of this layer.
Place other half of noodles on top of cheese mixture.
Top with the meat mixture.

Cover and refrigerate the casserole overnight or at least 6 hours before baking. Remove from refrigerator 1 hour before baking.

Recipe Continues...

80

GRETA'S PERFECT BEEF & PASTA CASSEROLE

Continued...

PREHEAT OVEN: 350 degrees F.

Place casserole in preheated oven and bake for 40 minutes. Remove from oven, garnish sides of casserole dish with the held over 1 cup of noodles. Melt the 1/2 cup butter and pour evenly over the noodle garnish. Cover with foil and bake another 20 minutes. Check casserole to make sure it is hot.

Remove from oven and garnish with pepper rings on top of casserole.

BONUS: Does not freeze well.

YIELD: 12 - 15 servings

THREE BEAN STEW
WITH VEGETABLES

As Marilyn remarks "this dish is for the vegetarians in your life, but for everyone who enjoys something good, different and easy!"

2 small carrots
2 small onions
1/2 cup stewed tomato
  pieces
2 pickled jalapeño peppers
  sliced (optional)
2 tablespoons vegetable oil
1 10-ounce package frozen
  corn kernels
1 16-ounce can black beans

1 16-ounce can red kidney
  beans
1 16-ounce can chick peas
1 4-ounce can chopped
  green chilies
1/4 cup Balsamic or sherry
  wine vinegar
Salt and freshly ground
  pepper

Chop the onions and tomatoes. Peel and slice the carrots 1/4-inch thick. Seed and mince the jalapeños for a hot and spicy taste.

Heat the oil in a medium size sauce pan over medium heat. Add the carrots and onions; reduce heat to low and simmer covered until somewhat tender, about 3 minutes. Add the tomatoes, jalapeños, corn (frozen or thawed), the beans with their juices and the green chilies, drained.

Recipe Continues...

THREE BEAN STEW WITH VEGETABLES
Continued...

Cover and simmer for as little as 20 minutes, just to heat the ingredients or for as long as 45 minutes for a mellow flavor.

Stir the beans to make certain they are not scorching.

BONUS: Marilyn says the beans are delicious over a bowl of pasta, or rice—her favorite. She uses DelMonte® brand Mexican tomatoes and if you like spicy, be sure to use the pickled jalapenos—sliced.

YIELD: 4 - 6 servings

REGAL BAKED STROGANOFF

This stroganoff is indeed convenient to make and impressive enough to serve to royalty.

2-1/2 pounds top round steak cut in strips 1/2-inch thick
3/4 cup vegetable oil
1 tablespoon salt
1/2 teaspoon pepper
1/4 cup dry red wine
1 cup small whole onions, peeled, or 1 large white onion, sliced
2 cups sliced fresh mushrooms

1/4 cup tomato paste
3 tablespoons flour
1 10-1/2-ounce can condensed consomme
1 bay leaf, crumbled
1 clove garlic, minced
1/2 cup low fat sour cream (optional)

Hot buttered noodles—homemade or purchased

Brown the meat quickly in vegetable oil, then transfer to a 3-quart casserole. Add salt, pepper and wine.

In the drippings in the frying pan, sauté onions until just golden brown; add mushrooms and cook 5 minutes.

Mix the tomato paste, flour and consomme; add to onions and mushrooms along with bay leaf and garlic. Mix well, then pour over meat.

Recipe Continues...

REGAL BAKED STROGANOFF

Continued...

Cover and bake in a 350 degree F. oven for 1 hour or until meat is fork tender. Remove casserole from oven and slowly stir in sour cream. Serve with hot buttered noodles.

BONUS: We like the stroganoff without the sour cream.
If you bake the stroganoff early in the day, hold the sour cream until you reheat the stroganoff for serving.

YIELD: 6 servings

CHICKEN AND BLACK BEAN ENCHILADAS

Defrost those Margaritas, put on your sombreros and prepare yourselves for a unique dinner of chicken and black beans—enchilada style. Don't forget to invite your best friends to join in this very distinctive fiesta. The siesta comes later!

1 pound skinless, boneless chicken breasts
3 slices lean bacon
2 cloves garlic, minced
1-1/2 cups picante sauce
1 16-ounce can black beans undrained

1 red bell pepper, chopped
1/2 teaspoon ground cumin
1/4 teaspoon salt
1/2 cup sliced green onions
12 flour tortillas (7-inch)
1-1/2 cups shredded Monterey Jack Cheese

TOPPINGS:

Shredded lettuce, chopped tomatoes, sour cream, guacamole

Cut chicken into short thin strips. Cook bacon in 10-inch skillet until crisp. Remove to paper towel to drain; crumble.

Pour off all but 2 tablespoons drippings. Sauté the chicken strips and garlic in drippings for 3 - 5 minutes. Stir in 1/2 cup picante sauce, beans, pepper, cumin and salt. Simmer 7 minutes or until thickened, stirring frequently.

Recipe Continues...

CHICKEN AND BLACK BEAN ENCHILADAS
Continued...

Stir in onions and bacon. Spoon heaping 1/4 cup of the chicken mixture down the center of each tortilla; top with 1 tablespoon of cheese. Roll up and place seam side down in a lightly greased 13" x 9" baking dish. Spoon remaining picante sauce over enchiladas.

BAKE at 350 degrees F. for 15 minutes. Top with remaining cheese and bake 3 minutes.

Add toppings as desired and serve with additional picante sauce.

YIELD: 6 servings

TACO STRATA OLÉ

Oven stratas are always fashionable for special festive occasions. This taco-like 24-hour strata is ideal for a Super Bowl party and can be prepared ahead of time.

10 slices whole wheat bread
2 cups fresh mushrooms, thinly sliced
1 cup sliced green onions including some of the tops
1 7-ounce can diced green chilies
3 cups shredded sharp cheddar cheese
4 large eggs
2 egg whites

2-1/2 cups 2% milk
1 tablespoon dried ground mustard
1 teaspoon ground cumin
1 tablespoon liquid hot pepper
Salt and pepper to taste

1 cup tortilla chips—crushed
Salsa—homemade or purchased

In an 8" x 10" casserole dish, layer one-half of the bread pieces; you may have to trim a little to fit. Save scraps.

Top bread with one-half of the sliced mushrooms, onions, chilies and cheddar cheese. Repeat layers starting again with the bread and scraps, ending with cheese.

Recipe Continues...

TACO STRATA OLÉ

Continued...

Beat the eggs and egg whites . Blend with the milk, mustard and hot pepper seasoning. Pour over bread mixture in casserole.

Cover dish and refrigerate 24 hours or at least 8 hours before baking.

PREHEAT OVEN 350 degrees F.

Before baking, uncover dish and scatter the crushed tortilla chips over all. Bake until golden or about 50 to 55 minutes.

Remove from oven, let stand for 15 minutes. Spoon out portions to guests and have salt and salsa nearby to complete the taco strata.

BONUS: Bev's Salsa from Volume 2 "Best of Friends, Too!" is an excellent go-along with the strata.

YIELD: 8 - 10 servings

CHICKEN FAJITAS BY DIXIE

This is the mexican dish mentioned in the "Bonus" to Dixie's Fresh Raspberry Pie recipe. The two served together become a dynamic duo. For your next Mexican food fiesta, be sure to include "CHICKEN FAJITAS BY DIXIE."

MARINADE:

1 clove garlic minced
1/2 teaspoons seasoning salt
1/2 teaspoons ground cumin
1/2 teaspoon chili powder

1/2 teaspoon red pepper flakes
2 tablespoons vegetable oil
2 tablespoons lemon juice

Combine all marinade ingredients and pour over:

2 halves of chicken breasts—cooked and cut into bite-size chunks. Marinate for 2 - 3 hours in refrigerator.

FAJITAS:

2 tablespoons vegetable oil
1/2 cup sliced onion
1/2 cup chopped green onions

3/4 cup sliced red bell pepper (1 small pepper)
1/2 cup sliced green bell pepper (1/2 pepper)

Recipe Continues...

CHICKEN FAJITAS BY DIXIE
Continued...

Sauté onions and peppers in oil until tender crisp. Add the marinated chicken and heat through.

4 flour tortillas for Fajitas (or 8-inch flour tortillas) Salsa	Sour cream Guacamole

Entice your guests to "build" their own Fajitas buffet-style. Place the warmed tortillas, Fajita stir-fry, and garnishes buffet-style. Serve fresh fruit and/or tossed fresh veggies along side. Don't forget the Margaritas and Dixie's Fresh Raspberry Pie for dessert! Dixie serves white rice and beans as a side dish.

BONUS: Recipe doubles or triples easily for more than 4 South-of-the-border guests.

P.S. If you get caught short-handed with no warning, most delis have prepared Fajita stir-fry in their repertoire. Of course, Dixie's is best.

YIELD: 4 servings

MEXICAN CHICKEN

Very tasty and if you fancy Mexican cuisine, this chicken dish is exemplary. The recipe comes from a "Best of Friends" pen pal, or I should say phone pal who also has written a cookbook. She, too, works in the "legal" world and some of her recipes are akin to mine. We seem to think, work and cook alike. Several of Marilyn's recipes appear in "Festive occasions," with her consent, of course.

3 whole chicken breasts, boned, skinned and split (I buy skinned, boneless chicken breasts to save time)
1-1/2 tablespoons butter
1-1/2 tablespoons oil
1/2 cup chopped onion
1 clove garlic, minced
2 stalks celery, thinly sliced
1 4-ounce can chopped green chilies
1 1-pound can stewed tomatoes
1/2 cup chicken broth (homemade or purchased)
1/4 teaspoon oregano leaves
1/2 teaspoon ground cumin
1/4 teaspoon granulated sugar
Salt and pepper to taste
1-1/2 cups shredded sharp cheddar cheese

Pound chicken breasts to 1/4-inch thickness. Heat butter and oil in oven proof fry pan over medium heat; brown chicken breasts 2 minutes on each side.

Recipe Continues...

92

MEXICAN CHICKEN
Continued...

Remove chicken from pan and set aside. Place onion, garlic and celery in fry pan; cook until onion is limp. Add chilies, stewed tomatoes, broth, cumin, oregano and sugar. Cook for 10 minutes. Season with salt and pepper. Place chicken back in pan and spoon tomato mixture over chicken and continue cooking for 20 minutes. Sprinkle with grated cheese; place under broiler until cheese melts.

BONUS: Good served alongside rice. Also, Marilyn likes a scoop of refried beans on the individual dinner plates, lettuce with guacamole dressing, and flour tortillas buttered, rolled, and heated.

A fresh fruit combination is also a possibility.

YIELD: 6 servings

CHICKEN LEMON SHELL QUICHE

Are you searching for something exciting, refreshing and unique to serve for early Sunday brunch? Try this lemon pastry shell filled with a delicate chicken filling. Poppyseed Bread and a fruit bowl will complete this elegant festivity.

CRUST:

1-1/2 cups all-purpose flour
1/2 teaspoon salt
3 tablespoons ice water
9 tablespoons butter (1 stick plus 1 tablespoon)

1 heaping teaspoon shortening
Grated rind and the juice of half a lemon

Sift flour and salt, cut in butter and shortening until crumbly. Add lemon rind, juice and cold water. Mix lightly. Form a ball, adding a small amount of extra flour, if needed. Roll out on lightly floured board. Roll 1/2 inches larger than a 10-inch pie plate. Roll edge of crust under and flute pastry on edge of pie plate. Prick bottom and sides of crust with fork.

BAKE at 425 degrees F. for 10 minutes. Crust will be only partially baked.

Recipe Continues...

94

CHICKEN LEMON SHELL QUICHE

Continued...

FILLING:

2 whole chicken breasts
   skinned, boned and cut
   into 1-inch cubes
1/2 teaspoon salt
1/4 teaspoon white pepper
1/4 cup corn oil
1 large onion, thinly sliced
   and separated into rings
1 large firm tomato, seeded,
   peeled and cut into
   cubes—drained

3 large eggs
3/4 cup 2% milk
3/4 cup half-and-half
4-1/2 to 5 ounces Gruyere or
   aged Swiss cheese, cut in
   small pieces
1/4 cup freshly grated
   Parmesan
Pinch of ground nutmeg
1 teaspoon butter, cut in
   pieces

Add 1/2 teaspoon salt and pepper to chicken. Sauté slowly, 5 to 6 minutes in heated oil. Remove chicken, add onion and cook until nearly tender. Add tomato, cover and cook 7 minutes or until moisture evaporates. Beat eggs. Add milk, cheeses, cream, nutmeg and remaining salt. Arrange onion, tomato and chicken on bottom of pastry shell. Pour in egg mixture and dot with butter. Bake in preheated 375 degree F. oven 35 to 40 minutes. If knife inserted 3 inches from side of pie plate comes out clean, quiche is done. Remove from oven and let stand 10 minutes before cutting.

Recipe Continues...

CHICKEN LEMON SHELL QUICHE
Continued...

SAUCE:

10 small fresh mushrooms,
   chopped
3 tablespoons butter
Salt and pepper to taste
2 tablespoons flour

1/2 cup half-and-half
2 tablespoons chutney
1/2 pint low fat sour cream
1/4 cup dry sherry

Sauté the chopped mushrooms in butter. Season with salt and pepper. Add flour and blend. Stir in cream and cook until thick, stirring constantly. Add chutney, sour cream and sherry. Heat through. Serve over sliced quiche.

BONUS: I chill the pie dough and roll out between two sheets of waxed paper. Run a knife around edge of rolled out dough and slowly peel waxed paper away.

YIELD: 8 slices with mushroom sauce

BREAKFAST PIZZA

The experts say that pizza is not all that bad for breakfast. Possibly better nourishment than no breakfast at all. I used to eat chocolate cake with old-fashioned cooked fudge frosting with cream poured over the top. My mother seemed to think this was better than "no breakfast" at all. Come to think of it, I could still handle that wonderful chocolate fudge frosting any time of the day!

1 pound bulk pork sausage   1 medium onion, chopped

Brown the sausage and onion; drain.

1 tube Crescent roll dough

(Separate triangles of dough and press onto 14-inch round pizza pan to cover surface and form a rim at edge).

PLACE THE FOLLOWING ON ROUND OF DOUGH:

The browned sausage and onions which have been drained.
1 to 2 cups shredded frozen hash browns, thawed.
one cup or more shredded sharp cheddar cheese.

Recipe Continues...

BREAKFAST PIZZA
Continued...

MIX TOGETHER:

5 eggs, beaten
1/4 cup 2% milk
1/2 teaspoon salt

1/4 teaspoon ground black
pepper

Pour over the covered round of dough.
Top with 3 tablespoons grated Parmesan cheese.

BAKE: 425 degrees F. 12 - 15 minutes or until crust is golden and cheese is melted.

BONUS: Other ingredients could be added, i.e., sliced black olives, chopped green pepper, sliced mushrooms, anything you like on other pizza would also be tasty for breakfast or brunch.

YIELD: 1 14-inch round pizza

BARCELONA PUFF

This very delicious Puff comes to "Festive Occasions" from a Bed and Breakfast Inn. You will definitely want to keep this Puff recipe handy for all seasons. It is fun to "build" and can be served any time of the day or night.

PREHEAT OVEN: 375 degrees F.

10 eggs
1/2 cup all-purpose flour
1 teaspoon baking powder
1/2 teaspoon salt
3/4 pound mixed Colby or
   Sharp cheddar shredded

1/2 stick (4 ounces) softened
   butter
1-1/2 pints Chivo (sour
   cream with chives)
1 4-ounce can green chilies

Beat the eggs, add next three ingredients. Mix in the butter, Chivo and chilies. Stir in the shredded cheese by hand.

Pour mixture into 2 buttered 9" pie plates.
Bake at 375 degrees F. for 30 to 35 minutes.

BONUS: Half of the recipe makes 6 servings. Full recipe serves 12 nicely. If you make the full recipe you can use a larger baking pan to bake the puff—although I prefer the pie plates.

YIELD: 12 servings

SUNDAY A.M. PANCAKES

Most kitchen cupboards have a package of pancake mix on hand for that special Sunday morning breakfast or brunch. If the cupboard is bare, here is the recipe you will never be without.

HEAT GRIDDLE OR OTHER PAN FOR
COOKING PANCAKES—325 degrees F.

1 heaping cup all purpose
   flour
2 teaspoons granulated
   sugar
1 teaspoon soda
1/4 teaspoon salt

1 tablespoon melted butter
   or margarine
2 large eggs—well beaten
1 cup low fat buttermilk
1/2 teaspoon vanilla

In a medium mixing bowl place all ingredients in the order given. If you have a whisk amongst your kitchen utensils, use it to mix together the pancake batter. Otherwise, use a spoon and mix batter until no lumps remain.

Cook pancakes on griddle until little bubbles appear on top. Turn over and cook until done. This does not take very long so watch that you don't burn them.

Serve with your favorite syrups and fresh fruits in season.

Recipe Continues...

SUNDAY A.M. PANCAKES
Continued...

BONUS: I add fresh huckleberries—about 1/2 cup. You can use any kind of berry available in your "neck of the woods." Drained, canned berries would also be a plus. And...don't leave out the vanilla. I didn't test using egg substitute but I see no reason why it wouldn't be favorable. (My cholesteral is 104 so I don't have to worry about such things as "eggs." Aren't I the lucky one!!!!?)

YIELD: 14 - 16 medium pancakes

SINFULLY CHOCOLATE WAFFLES

My craving for chocolate brings this absolutely fabulous recipe to my best of friends (and probably a few "unfriendlies," too). When I received the recipe from a friend, I thought chocolate waffles were going a bit far...wrong—they are the BEST waffles I have ever had the privilege to savor. Need I tell you more!!!?

2 cups all purpose flour
4 teaspoons baking powder
1 teaspoon salt
3 tablespoons sugar
3 teaspoons cocoa

2 egg yolks
1-1/2 cups low fat milk

1 teaspoon Mapeline
   flavoring
4 tablespoons vegetable oil

2 egg whites, beaten until
   soft peaks form

MAPELINE SYRUP:

2 cups granulated sugar
1 cup water

1/2 teaspoon mapeline
   flavoring

Mix together and bring to boil. Serve warm with waffles

SINFULLY CHOCOLATE WAFFLES
Continued...

WAFFLE BATTER:

In a large mixing bowl, add the dry ingredients and stir to mix well. Add the 2 egg yolks, milk, Mapeline flavoring and oil. Mix well. Gently fold in the 2 beaten egg whites and bake in waffle iron as you would any other waffle.

SERVE with the Mapeline syrup or syrup of your choice. I spoon fresh fruit on top; then a little mapeline syrup on top of the fruit.

BONUS: This recipe is an old family favorite of my friend Sharon Knudson—her mother who is now 94 took the recipe from a Mapeline box before Sharon was born—it's old—but we aren't telling just how old are we Sharon?

YIELD: 6 to 8 waffles

FRENCH DIP

A new twist on an old recipe. Most menus still include this staple. Try it on your own at home Jeanne's way. Your friends will appreciate its modification.

3 to 4 pound boneless rump roast	1 cup chopped celery
1 cup chopped carrots	1 or 2 packages au jus mix—your favorite brand
1 cup chopped onion	

Place roast in large roaster with a tight fitting lid. Cover roast with the chopped vegies. Add <u>no</u> liquid.

Bake covered at 350 degrees F. 3 to 4 hours. Remove from oven and place meat on carving board to cool. Transfer the cooked vegies to blender and blend until smooth. Prepare au jus in roaster adding the blended vegies.

When beef has cooled, slice into thin slices; add to au jus.

For serving place slice of beef on French bun and spoon au jus into small bowls or cups for dipping.

BONUS: Use as many packages of au jus as you want to have an adequate amount for however many persons you intend to feed. Also, I add a little red wine to the au jus—this is optional of course. Also, if you have an electric knife, it works great for slicing the beef.

YIELD: Depends on how many slices of beef you get from the roast

KAY'S TENDERIZER
FOR SIRLOIN

Adapted for outdoor cookery, this marinade can be used for most cuts of beef. Kay likes to use it for her marvelous top sirloin beef entreé. Best of all, it's easy. The 4th of July comes to mind for this recipe. Add to your menu with a refreshing potable and a chocolate dessert.

2 pound top sirloin steak—
have butcher cut it 2
inches thick

3/4 cup vegetable oil
6 tablespoons low sodium
soy sauce
2 tablespoons
Worcestershire

1 tablespoon dry mustard
1 teaspoon salt
1/4 cup wine vinegar
1 teaspoon dried parsley
1/3 cup lemon juice
1 clove garlic, crushed
1/2 teaspoon black pepper

Combine all ingredients in a glass jar. May be made ahead and saved. Marinate beef at least 4 hours turning frequently. Marinade should cover beef. Cook as desired but I suggest grilling it on the barbecue.

–NOTES–

DESSERTS:

DESSERTS
Index

INCREDIBLE PIE CRUST!

So unpretentious is this pie crust, it can be accomplished in the dark. I know this to be a fact because as I was testing the pie dough, our lights went out and I completed the dough making and formed pie crusts by candlelight. I thought my cleanup was spectacular until the next morning when I viewed the kitchen. It appeared that the "troops" had passed through in the quiet of the night.

2 cups all purpose flour	2/3 cup (scant) vegetable oil
1/2 teaspoon salt	1/3 cup cold water
1/2 teaspoon baking powder	

In a medium-large covered plastic bowl such as Rubbermaid® or Tupperware®, place the flour, salt and baking powder; stir just to blend. Add the vegetable oil and water, place the lid on tightly and shake about four times (ceiling to floor motion), remove lid and like magic the dough is ready to roll. You may want to stir a few times using your hands to "pick" up any little crumbs that didn't form into the ball of dough.

Divide the dough in two pieces. Place each one between waxed paper and roll out to the size you want. The recipe will make two 8-inch crusts perfectly. I have stretched the dough to make 2 9-inch crusts.

Recipe Continues...

INCREDIBLE PIE CRUST!

Continued...

Proceed according to specific recipe directions.

BONUS:

For recipes using a baked pie crust, heat oven to 425 degrees F. Prick bottom and sides thoroughly with a fork (about 40 times) to prevent shrinkage. Bake at 425 degrees F. for 10 to 15 minutes or until just golden.

For recipes using a double crust, transfer bottom crust to pie plate. Trim edge evenly with edge of pie plate. I use my kitchen shears. Moisten pastry edge with water. I use a pastry brush or my index finger dipped in cold water. Add desired filling to unbaked pie crust. Lift top crust onto filled pie. Trim 1/2 inch beyond edge of pie plate. Fold top edge under bottom crust, flute edge. Be sure to cut slits in top crust to allow steam to escape. Bake according to specific recipe directions.

YIELD: 2 crusts

STRAWBERRY CHOCOLATE MERINGUES

Always a tempting dessert to make and to serve. Not too sweet and the meringue is so much fun to work with. Simply simple and luscious in its content.

3 large egg whites
1 teaspoon almond extract
1/2 teaspoon baking powder
3/4 cup semisweet chocolate pieces
1/2 cup chopped pecans
3-3/4 cup granulated sugar

1 cup crushed rich round crackers (23 or so)
1 cup whipping cream
2 tablespoons sifted powdered sugar
1/2 teaspoon vanilla extract
2 cups ripe sliced strawberries

Combine the egg whites, almond extract and baking powder in a large mixer bowl. Let stand at room temperature for 10 minutes.

In the meantime, mix 2 tablespoons of the chocolate pieces with 2 tablespoons of the pecans; reserve this for the garnish.

Coarsely chop remaining chocolate and finely chop remaining pecans. Combine and set aside.

Beat egg white mixture with an electric mixer on medium speed until soft peaks form. Add the sugar, 1 tablespoon at a time, beating on high speed until very stiff peaks form.

Recipe Continues...

STRAWBERRY CHOCOLATE MERINGUES
Continued...

In a medium mixer bowl, combine the coarsely chopped chocolate and pecan mixture and the crushed crackers. Fold cracker mixture into egg whites. Spread meringue into a greased 9-inch pie plate, building up the sides.

BAKE in a 350 degree F. oven about 25 minutes or till top is golden. Cool completely. In a medium mixing bowl, combine the whipping cream, powdered sugar and vanilla extract. Beat on low speed until soft peaks form. Fold in 1-1/2 cups of the sliced strawberries; spoon atop cooled meringue.

Top with remaining strawberries and reserved chocolate; spoon atop cooled meringue.

Top with remaining strawberries and reserved chocolate pecan mixture. Serve immediatly or chill for up to 24 hours.

YIELD: 8 servings

APPLE UPSIDE DOWN PIE

If you make pineapple upside down cake, you know how good it is. This upside down apple pie is not of the traditional variety. You can use ready-made pie crusts to simplify the recipe, but I use my own recipe. The choice is yours. See "Best of Friends, Etc."

PREHEAT OVEN: 425 degrees F.

GLAZE:

- 1/4 cup firmly packed brown sugar
- 1 tablespoon light corn syrup
- 1 tablespoon butter or margarine melted
- 1/2 cup pecan halves

Two pie crusts (top and bottom)

PIE FILLING:

- 2/3 cup granulated sugar
- 2 tablespoons all purpose flour
- 1/2 teaspoon cinnamon
- 1/4 teaspoon nutmeg— freshly ground is best
- 4 cups sliced, peeled Granny Smith apples

Whipped cream for garnish

In a 9-inch pie plate, combine the brown sugar, corn syrup and melted butter; spread evenly over bottom of pie plate. Arrange pecans over this mixture.

Recipe Continues...

APPLE UPSIDE DOWN PIE

Continued...

In a small bowl, combine the granulated sugar, 2 tablespoons flour and spices; mix well. Arrange half of the apple slices in pie crust-lined pie plate; sprinkle with half of the sugar mixture. Repeat with the remaining apple slices and sugar mixture. Top with the second crust; seal and flute. Cut slits in several places of the crust.

BAKE: 425 degrees F. for 8 minutes. Reduce oven temperature to 375 degrees F. Bake another 24 to 30 minutes or until apples are tender and crust is just golden. Remove pie from oven, loosen edge of pie; carefully invert onto serving plate. Serve warm or cold with whipped cream or ice cream.

BONUS: FOR BAKING, I PLACE PIE ON A FOIL LINED COOKIE SHEET TO GUARD AGAINST SPILLAGE. BE CAREFUL WHEN YOU TURN PIE OUT OF PIE PLATE ONTO SERVING DISH - CARAMEL SAUCE IS HOT.

YIELD: 8 servings

DIXIE'S FRESH RASPBERRY PIE

Dixie once again shares one of her mouth-watering recipes with "Best of Friends" cookbooks. We had the distinct pleasure of experiencing this raspberry pie with fresh raspberries from Dixie's own garden. Indubitably guaranteed to satisfy!

PREHEAT OVEN: 350 degrees F.

DIXIE'S OWN CRUST:

1/3 cup granulated sugar
1-1/2 cups all-purpose flour
1/2 cup real butter (not
   light)

3 ounces softened cream
   cheese

Place all ingredients (EXCEPT CREAM CHEESE) in medium mixing bowl and "knead" with hand until blended. Pat into bottom and sides of a 10-inch pie pan. Bake 20 minutes or until golden. Remove crust from oven and cool.

Spread the softened cream cheese on bottom of cooled crust.

Recipe Continues...

DIXIE'S FRESH RASPBERRY PIE
Continued...

RASPBERRY GLAZE:

1 cup granulated sugar	2 tablespoons cornstarch
	1 cup cool water

In a medium sauce pan, combine the sugar and cornstarch; add the water and cook over medium heat until sauce is clear and thick. Stir the mixture during the cooking process. Remove from heat, add 2 tablespoons raspberry Jello powder and stir well. Cool mixture.

1 to 1-1/2 quarts fresh raspberries

Meanwhile, place 1 or 1-1/2 quarts fresh raspberries in a bowl, and pour cooled glaze over to coat the berries well. Pour into cooled pastry shell.

Chill pie and serve with a dollop of whipped cream on top of each slice.

BONUS: Doesn't this just make those saliva glands work overtime? As soon as you see fresh raspberries on the bush or at the Farmers Market—lay everything aside and get to your kitchen. The crust is easy and doesn't have to be rolled out. There are no excuses for not creating this dessert for your family and friends soon. It is a perfect dessert to serve with "Chicken Fajitas by Dixie" to be found elsewhere in "Festive Occasions."

YIELD: 6 - 8 servings

NORBYS' STRAWBERRY PIE

This delicious and easy-to-prepare strawberry pie comes to "Best of Friends" from Norbys of Aberdeen. They wanted to share their favorite strawberry pie with "Best of Friends" and I, for one, am delighted to include it in "Festive Occasions." I can verify that this is a very simple recipe, yet it packs a whole lot of flavor into its simplicity.

PREHEAT OVEN: 375 degrees F.

CRUST:

1 cup all-purpose flour
1/3 cup margarine

2 tablespoons granulated
   sugar
1 egg yolk

In a mixing bowl, mix the first three ingredients together. Work the egg yolk into the mixture by hand. Press the mixture into a buttered 9-inch pie tin and bake for 12 minutes at 375 degrees F.

Recipe Continues...

NORBYS' STRAWBERRY PIE

Continued...

Meanwhile, mix together in a medium saucepan:

1 package strawberry flavored Danish Dessert (from the Jello and pudding section of your favorite grocery store)	2 cups water 1/2 cup granulated sugar

Cook mixture until thickened. Pour mixture over 4 cups fresh strawberries which have been placed on the cooled crust. Refrigerate for at least 2 hours before serving.

SERVING: Spoon a bit of whipped cream on top of each slice of pie.

WARNING! This is a very refreshing dessert.

BONUS: We liked the crust so much that the second time I made the pie, I doubled the crust ingredients so that we had more crust to go along with those big fresh strawberries.

YIELD: 6 - 8 small portions

HUCKLEBERRY BOG

Huckleberries or blueberries make this dessert extraordinary!
Simply use your microwave to create this magical dessert.
Plan to dazzle your family and friends soon.

4 cups huckleberries
1 cup granulated sugar
(or more if berries are not
real sweet)

1/4 teaspoon freshly ground
nutmeg

Place berries in microwave-safe bowl. Stir in sugar and nutmeg.
Microwave on high for 5 - 6 minutes or until berry mixture is very
hot and juicy.

Remove from microwave.

DUMPLINGS:

2 cups biscuit mix (such as
Bisquick®)
2 tablespoons granulated
sugar

2/3 cup 2% milk
1 tablespoon melted butter

Place biscuit mix, sugar, milk and melted butter in mixing bowl. Stir
until well blended. If too thick, add more milk; if too thin, add more
biscuit mix. Batter should be just thick enough to hold its shape
when dropped on top of hot mixture.

Recipe Continues...

HUCKLEBERRY BOG

Continued...

Drop dumpling mixture by spoon on top of hot mixture. Return to microwave and cook 5 - 6 minutes or until dumplings feel "dry." You can determine if the dumplings are cooked by touching tops. If they are still "sticky" to the touch, microwave another minute or so.

Remove from microwave, allow to cool a bit. To serve, spoon individual servings into bowls with dumpling on bottom, berry sauce next and top with a scoop of vanilla ice cream.

BONUS: For a smaller crowd, the recipe can be cut in half.

YIELD: 6 - 8 servings

BERTIE'S FAVORITE CARROT CAKE

There are many carrot cake recipes in existence and most of them are tasty. However, Bertie has added her personal touch to this recipe and that is why it has become my favorite, too. The "Garden Nibblers" also think it is pretty special!

PREHEAT OVEN: 350 degrees F.
You will need 3 8-inch round or square cake pans.

2-1/2 cups all purpose flour
2 cups granulated sugar
2 teaspoons baking soda
1/2 teaspoon salt
2 teaspoons ground
    cinnamon
1/4 teaspoon freshly ground
    nutmeg

1-1/2 cups Canola or other
    vegetable cooking oil
4 eggs

3 cups finely shredded
    carrots
1 cup chopped pecans

Combine the first six ingredients in a large mixer bowl. Add the oil and eggs and beat with electric mixer until well mixed. Stir in the shredded carrots and chopped pecans. Pour batter into three greased and floured cake pans. Bake for 30 or 35 minutes or until cake tester comes out pristine. Remove from oven and place on rack to cool.

Recipe Continues...

BERTIE'S FAVORITE CARROT CAKE

Continued...

FROSTING:

1 8-ounce package cream
   cheese, softened
1/2 cup margarine or butter,
   softened

2 teaspoons vanilla extract
4 to 4-1/2 cups powdered
   sugar, sifted

Beat together the cream cheese, margarine and vanilla until light and fluffy. Gradually add 2 cups powdered sugar, beating well. Add enough of the remaining sugar until frosting reaches spreading consistency.

BONUS: Bertie spreads orange marmalade on the tops of the two bottom layers while they are still a little warm. Then she frosts over them with the cream cheese frosting. The marmalade is the personal touch that makes this carrot cake so special.

This cake freezes perfectly so it is a good one to make ahead of time and have on hand for an extra-special "festive occasion." I like to serve the cake at Easter.

YIELD: 12 - 14 servings

M.M.'S POPPY SEED CAKE

An unusually moist poppy seed cake, this is the best of the many cake recipes I have tested. Try this one soon. I know you will agree with my judgment.

PREHEAT OVEN: 350 degrees F.

1 package white cake mix
1 small package vanilla
  instant-pudding
4 eggs
1/2 cup Canola or other
  vegetable oil
1 cup cold water
1/4 cup poppy seeds
2 teaspoons vanilla extract

2 tablespoons granulated
  sugar
1 teaspoon cinnamon
2 teaspoons unsweetened
  cocoa

In large mixer bowl, add the first seven ingredients. Blend on medium speed about 3 minutes. Hold aside.

In small bowl, mix together the granulated sugar, cinnamon and cocoa.

In 12-cup greased and floured Bundt pan pour in three-fourths of the cake batter. Spoon or sprinkle the sugar mixture evenly on top of this layer and then add the remaining batter.

Recipe Continues...

M.M.'S POPPY SEED CAKE
Continued...

Bake 45 - 50 minutes or until tester comes out au naturel.

Cool on wire rack before removing from pan.

BONUS: I like to add about 1/4 cup Banana Liqueur to the batter. You can reduce the water by that amount if you choose, but I just add the liqueur along with the 1 cup water. Also I make a lemon glaze to pour over the cake while it is still warm. (About 2 cups powdered sugar and enough lemon juice to make a thin glaze).

CHOCOLATE TORTILLA TORTE

This dessert torte is unique and uncomplicated. "It looks and tastes gourmet but is so easy! This is a fabulous finish to a buffet style meal of Tacos!" You will want to experiment with this soon so don't forget the flour tortillas the next time you do your grocery shopping.

1 6-ounce package semi-sweet chocolate bits
2 cups (1 pint) low fat sour cream
3 tablespoons confectioner's sugar

4 flour tortillas—10 inch
1 to 2 ounces milk chocolate—shaved for garnish

Pour semi-sweet chocolate bits into top of double boiler. Add 1 cup of the sour cream and 1 tablespoon confectioner's sugar. Heat over simmering water, stirring until chocolate melts. Place pan of sauce in cold water to cool, stirring occasionally.

Set one of the flour tortillas on serving plate and spread evenly with one-third of the chocolate mixture. Cover with another tortilla, another third of the sauce and the last tortilla. Make pile as level as possible.

Recipe Continues...

CHOCOLATE TORTILLA TORTE
Continued...

Blend the remaining sour cream with the remaining 2 tablespoons confectioner's sugar and spread evenly over top and sides of the torte. Chill, covered with a large inverted bowl, at least 8 hours or as long as overnight.

Shave milk chocolate bar into curls using a vegetable peeler; pile chocolate curls on top of tortilla torte. To serve, cut in slim wedges with a very sharp knife.

BONUS: I prepare this torte early in the morning before I go to work. It is perfectly formed for guests at 7 p.m. dinner. It makes a great Wednesday eve dessert.

YIELD: 12 servings

CHOCOLATE FUDGE SURPRISE

A cake made famous by Pillsbury®, this is very similar to a prize-winning recipe that I served over 25 years ago. It will definitely be new to many of you.

You will need either a 12-cup fluted tube pan or 10-inch tube pan to complete this recipe. Also nuts are a requirement for a perfect cake.

PREHEAT OVEN: 350 degrees F.

1-3/4 cups granulated sugar
1-3/4 cups softened butter
  or margarine
6 eggs
2 cups confectioner's sugar

2-1/4 cups all purpose flour
3/4 cup unsweetened cocoa
2 cups chopped walnuts—
  a must

CHOCOLATE GLAZE:

3/4 cup confectioner's sugar
1/4 cup unsweetened cocoa

4 to 6 tablespoons 2% milk

Grease and flour cake pan—use "Baker's Joy" baking spray if available.

Recipe Continues...

CHOCOLATE FUDGE SURPRISE

Continued...

In a large bowl, combine the sugar and butter or margarine; beat until light and fluffy. Add eggs 1 at a time, beating very well after each addition.

Gradually add 2 cups confectioner's sugar; blend well. Lightly spoon flour into measuring cup; level off with knife.

By hand stir in flour and remaining cake ingredients, INCLUDING THE NUTS, until well blended.

Spoon batter into your choice of pans which has been greased and floured. Spread batter evenly.

BAKE: 350 Degrees F. 58 to 62 minutes

Remove from oven, cool on rack for at least 60 minutes. Invert onto serving plate and cool completely.

GLAZE:

In small bowl, blend 3/4 cup confectioner's sugar, 1/4 cup cocoa and enough milk for desired drizzling consistency. Spoon over entire top of cake, allowing some to run down the sides.
Store cake tightly covered.
BONUS: Above 3500 feet increase the flour to 2-1/4 cups plus 3 tablespoons. Completed cake has a soft filling so accurate oven temperature and baking time are essential to the success of this chocolate dessert.

YIELD: 16 servings

COWBOY 7-GRAIN COOKIES

Almost a complete breakfast in themselves, these cowboy cookies utilize my good friend's new "Cream of the West" roasted 7-grain cereal.

PREHEAT OVEN: 375 degrees F.

1-1/4 cups shortening or
   margarine
3/4 cup brown sugar

1/2 cup granulated sugar
2 eggs
1 teaspoon vanilla

In a large mixer bowl cream the shortening and sugars; add 2 eggs one at a time and the vanilla.

ADD AND BEAT:

1-1/2 cups all purpose flour
1 teaspoon baking soda
1-1/2 cups uncooked "Cream
   of the West 7-Grain
   cereal"

1 cup chocolate chips
1 cup Reese's Peanut
   Butter Pieces

Drop by rounded teaspoon on lightly greased cookie sheet. Bake at 375 degrees F. for 8 - 10 minutes. DO NOT OVERBAKE.

Recipe Continues...

COWBOY 7-GRAIN COOKIES

Continued...

Remove to rack for cooling before storing.

BONUS: If you can't find "Cream of the West" cereals, you can substitute oatmeal.

YIELD: 36 cookies

STELLA'S OATMEAL COOKIES

The only oatmeal cookies that Stella's family will eat. Your family most certainly will agree that they are "the" cookie voted most likely to succeed.

PREHEAT OVEN: 375 degrees F.

1 cup shortening or
  margarine or butter
1 cup granulated sugar
2 cups all purpose flour
2 cups oatmeal
1/2 cup 2% milk
1 teaspoon cinnamon

1 cup raisins (black or
  yellow)
1 cup walnuts chopped
2 eggs
1/2 teaspoon soda
1/2 teaspoon baking powder
1/2 teaspoon salt

In large mixer bowl, cream the shortening and sugar; add eggs. Sift dry ingredients and add to the creamed mixture. Add milk and mix well. Mix in oatmeal. Stir in nuts and raisins.

Drop by teaspoon on lightly greased cookie sheet. Bake at 365 degrees F. for about 15 minutes or until golden. Remove cookies to a baking rack to cool for storage.

BONUS: Stella says you can add one 6-ounce package chocolate chips if desired.

P.S. I added 1 teaspoon of vanilla extract to the recipe. I used chocolate chips in half of the batter so I had some of each. We didn't have leftovers, but they will freeze nicely.

❧

TURTLE COOKIES

Many "turtle" recipes survive, but some are better than others. This is one of the "others" you will not want to pass up. They are chewy and should be enjoyed the first day of creating.

PREHEAT OVEN: 375 degrees F.

2-1/2 cups all purpose flour
3/4 cup unsweetened cocoa
1 teaspoon baking soda
1 cup granulated sugar
1 cup firmly packed brown sugar
1 cup butter, softened (or margarine)
2 teaspoons vanilla extract

2 eggs
1 cup chopped pecans
48 Rolo® Caramels in milk chocolate (9-ounce package)
2 tablespoons sugar
4 ounces vanilla-flavored candy coating for garnish

In small bowl, beat granulated sugar, brown sugar and butter until light and fluffy. Add vanilla and eggs; beat well. Add flour mixture (first three ingredients;) blend well. Stir in one-half cup of pecans. For each cookie, with floured hands, shape about 1 tablespoon dough around 1 caramel candy, covering completely.

In small bowl, combine remaining one-half cup pecans and 2 tablespoons sugar. Press one side of each ball into pecan mixture. Place nut side up, 2 inches apart on ungreased cookie sheets.

Recipe Continues...

TURTLE COOKIES
Continued...

BAKE at 375 degrees F. for 7 to 8 minutes, or until set and slightly cracked. Cool about 2 minutes, remove from cookie sheets, cool completely on wire rack.

WHITE CHOCOLATE COATING:

Melt candy coating (can use white chocolate chips) over low heat, stirring constantly until smooth. Drizzle over cookies for that "easy and elegant" expression.

BONUS: If the vanilla "drizzle" is not thin enough, add just a bit of margarine or butter to thin it.

Also, if you live high above the world (above 3,500 feet) increase flour to 2-3/4 cups—then complete recipe as written.

YIELD: 36 - 48 cookies

❧

DIVINELY DECADENT BROWNIES

Suffice it to say that these Brownies are not for the "fat" conscious. The butter and eggs make them "divinely decadent." Pursue these brownies at your own risk!

PREHEAT OVEN: 350 degrees F.

2 cups granulated sugar
1 cup butter
1/2 cup unsweetened cocoa
4 eggs
1 cup all purpose flour
1/2 teaspoon cinnamon

1/8 teaspoon freshly grated nutmeg
2 teaspoons vanilla extract
1/2 cup chopped pecans or walnuts

Grease 9 x 13-inch baking pan.

Cream the sugar and butter. Add eggs one at a time. Blend in the Cocoa, flour and spices which have been "mixed together in a separate bowl." Stir in vanilla and the nuts.

Turn into the greased pan and bake about 30 minutes or until the brownies start to "pull away" from the edges of the pan.
Cut while hot.

BONUS: Your favorite frosting can be "drizzled" over the baked brownies—of course, at your own risk........

P.S. Margarine and egg substitute can be used but the "real things in life" are best.

YIELD: 24 - 36 squares—depending on size desired

SPELL-BINDER COOKIES

This oatmeal-laced cookie recipe comes from a "Best of Friends" reader. Loaded with lots of goodies, you will not recognize it as "just any old cookie." It is a spell binder for sure.
Thanks Helen for a fresh outlook on oatmeal cookies.

PREHEAT OVEN: 375 degrees F.

1 cup margarine, softened
1 cup brown sugar—firmly packed

1 large egg
1 teaspoon vanilla extract

1-1/2 cups all purpose flour
1-1/2 teaspoons baking powder
1 teaspoon baking soda
1/2 teaspoon ground ginger

1 cup quick cooking oatmeal flakes
1 cup flaked coconut
1 cup salted Spanish peanuts
1/2 cup finely crushed Cornflakes cereal

In a large mixer bowl, place margarine. Gradually add brown sugar to the margarine, creaming until light and fluffy. Add the egg and vanilla; beat well. Combine the flour, baking powder, baking soda and ginger in a small bowl. Gradually add dry ingredients to cookie dough, blending well after each addition.

Recipe Continues...

135

SPELL-BINDER COOKIES
Continued...

Stir in oatmeal, coconut, peanuts and cornflakes. Drop by rounded teaspoonfuls onto ungreased cookie sheets. Bake at 375 degrees F. for about 10 to 12 minutes or until golden. Do not overbake.

BONUS: This makes a goodly amount of cookies. Freeze what you don't consume directly from the cookie sheets.

YIELD: 4 dozen cookies

CHOCOLATE CANDY KISS COOKIES

Made with everyone's favorite chocolate candy kisses, these cookies have been around our kitchen for many years. They seem to be a part of the family tree. "Best of Friends" is including the recipe just in case it may have blown off your tree.

PREHEAT OVEN: 375 degrees F.

1-3/4 cups all purpose flour
1/2 cup granulated sugar
1/2 cup brown sugar, firmly
   packed
1/2 teaspoon salt
1 teaspoon baking soda
1/2 cup shortening

1/2 cup peanut butter
2 tablespoons milk
1 teaspoon vanilla extract
1 large egg

Sugar
48 chocolate candy kisses

In a large mixer bowl combine flour, granulated sugar, brown sugar, baking soda, salt, shortening, peanut butter, milk, vanilla and egg. Beat at low speed until a stiff dough forms.

Recipe Continues...

CHOCOLATE CANDY KISS COOKIES
Continued...

Form a rounded teaspoonful of dough into a one-inch ball and roll in sugar. Place on ungreased cookie sheets about 2 inches apart. Bake for 10 to 12 minutes until light golden brown. Remove from oven and without wasting a second—immediately place a candy kiss on top of each cookie, pressing down firmly enough so that cookie cracks around the edge.

BONUS: Try the chocolate/almond kisses—they are new since this cookie recipe was born.

YIELD: 48 cookies—give or take

LEMON ICE BOX DESSERT

This recipe from Pat Erickson dates back from China 1943-44 when her father got the original recipe from Lawsing Buck (Pearl Buck the authoress' first husband). The recipe has travelled the world over. Although it is not a "lo-cal dessert, it is good and simple to double, triple, etc. for large gatherings."

1 cup graham cracker or vanilla wafer crumbs	2 eggs—separated
1 cup whipping cream	1 cup granulated sugar
	1/4 cup fresh lemon juice

Use old-fashioned aluminum ice-cube trays without the dividers for ease in freezing and serving or you can use one 8" x 8" square pan if preferred. That requires doubling the recipe.

Place half of the crumbs in the bottom of the ice cube tray or pan. Set aside.

Whip cream very stiff and add 1/2 cup granulated sugar. After washing beaters, in another bowl whip the egg whites until stiff. Fold in whipped egg yolks and remaining sugar.

Recipe Continues...

LEMON ICE BOX DESSERT

Continued...

Combine cream and egg mixtures. Gently fold in the lemon juice evenly throughout the mixture. Pour into prepared ice-cube tray, sprinkle top with remaining crumbs and freeze for 2 hours or over night, covered to protect against outside odors or flavors seeping into the dessert

BONUS: Easy to double or triple for more guests.

YIELD: 6-8 servings

LIME SQUARES

A new version of a time-honored lemony square cookie. The lime takes on a new flavor in this basic lemon bar cookie. I presume you will come to the same conclusion as I—it is a welcome transformation.

PREHEAT OVEN: 350 degrees F.

If you have a food processor—use it to assemble these refreshing lime bars.

1 cup all purpose flour
1/4 cup firmly packed
   brown sugar
1/2 teaspoon salt

6 tablespoons chilled
   unsalted butter—cut into
   pieces
1/2 cup toasted slivered
   almonds

FILLING:

3/4 cup granulated sugar
2 eggs
3 tablespoons fresh
   squeezed lime juice

1 tablespoon grated
   lime peel
1/2 teaspoon baking powder
Pinch of salt

Powdered sugar
Lime-peel curls (optional)

Line 8-inch square baking pan with foil. Butter foil.

Recipe Continues...

LIME SQUARES

Continued...

Mix the flour, sugar and salt in processor. Add butter and nuts and blend until fine meal forms. Press into the bottom of prepared pan. Bake until light brown—about 20 minutes.

Meanwhile blend 3/4 cup sugar, eggs, lime juice, 1 tablespoon grated lime peel, baking powder and salt in processor until smooth.

Pour filling onto hot crust. Bake until filling begins to brown and is springy to the touch—about 20 minutes. Remove from oven and cool on wire rack.

Lift foil and cookies from pan. Gently peel the foil from edges. Cut into 16 squares. (you can prepare a day ahead).

Wrap tightly and refrigerate. Sift powdered sugar over the cookies and garnish with lime peel if desired. Best served at room temperature.

BONUS: Best served day of baking. Wrap individually if you are fortunate enough to have a few remaining "crumbs" laying about.

YIELD: 16 squares

142

PEANUT BUTTER CHOCOLATE CHIP COOKIES

Another breed of chocolate chip cookies—these incorporate peanut butter—the world's favorite diversion.

PREHEAT OVEN: 350 degrees F.

1-1/2 cups all purpose flour
1 teaspoon baking soda
1/4 teaspoon salt
1/2 cup sweet butter, room temperature
1/2 cup packed light brown sugar
1/2 cup granulated sugar

1 egg
1 teaspoon vanilla extract
1/2 cup smooth peanut butter
1 ounce square unsweetened chocolate
1 cup semisweet chocolate morsels

Sift together first three ingredients. Use an electric mixer to cream the butter until light and fluffy. Add brown sugar and granulated sugar. Beat until fluffy; mix in the egg and vanilla, then peanut butter and melted chocolate. Mix in the flour and other dry ingredients. Stir in the chocolate morsels.

Form dough into 1-inch balls. Arrange on ungreased baking sheets, spaced about 1 - 2 inches apart. Flatten to 1/2 inch with back of fork in crosshatch pattern. Bake until the cookies are firm around edges and bottoms are browned. This should take about 12 minutes. Cool on wire rack. Store in airtight container.

YIELD: Makes about 36 cookies

ORANGE BISCOTTI WITH PISTACHIOS

Biscotti is an Italian treat delicious served with a sweet wine or other mid-day beverage. My first experience with biscotti was at an open house where it was served with a fruity red wine. It was suggested that I dip the biscotti in the wine to fully savor the "crunchy" consistency of the "biscuit." It was excellent advice. Try it.

1 cup granulated sugar	3-1/3 cups all purpose flour
4 eggs	2 teaspoons baking powder
2 tablespoons grated orange rind	3/4 cup finely chopped pistachios
2 tablespoons vegetable oil	Vegetable cooking spray
2 teaspoons vanilla extract	

Combine sugar and eggs in a large bowl; beat at high speed of an electric mixer until thick and light in color. This should take about 5 minutes.

Add orange rind, oil and vanilla extract. Beat until very well blended.

Combine flour, baking powder and pistachios; gradually add to the egg mixture, beating well. Cover and freeze the dough for about 30 minutes or until firm.

Recipe Continues...

ORANGE BISCOTTI WITH PISTACHIOS
Continued...

Turn dough out onto a lightly floured surface; divide into 4 equal parts. Shape each into a 10-inch long roll. Place cookie rolls about 2 inches apart on a large cookie sheet coated with cooking spray and flatten each roll to 3/4 inch thickness.

Bake at 325 degrees F. for 25 minutes or until wooden pick inserted in center of rolls comes out clean. (Cookie rolls will probably spread while baking). Remove from cookie sheets to wire rack. Cool 5 minutes.

Slice each roll diagonally into 18 1/2-inch thick slices. Place slices, cut sides down, on cookie sheets and bake again at
300 degrees F. for 15 minutes; turn cookies over and bake another 10 minutes or until dry. Cool on wire racks.

BONUS: I prefer a chocolate frosting-glaze on the biscotti after they are cooled. However, they are delicious without.

YIELD: 72 cookies

—NOTES—

SIGNIFICANT OTHERS:

SIGNIFICANT OTHERS
Index

SPECIALIZED LEMON CURD

Lemon curd is great to have on hand and this particular curd is delicious beyond any I have ever had the occasion to enjoy!!!

12 large egg yolks, lightly
   beaten and strained
1 cup fresh lemon juice
2ᶜ SUGAR

1 cup unsalted butter—room
   temperature
2 tablespoons grated lemon
   peel

In a large saucepan combine the sugar and egg yolks. Gradually stir in the lemon juice. Cook over medium low heat, stirring constantly until mixture coats the back of a metal spoon and the temperature reaches 168 degrees on a candy thermometer. Do not permit the mixture to reach boiling.

Remove from heat and using a whisk, lightly beat the mixture until a bit cooled. Gently stir in the butter.

While the lemon curd is barely warm, pour into sterilized jars, tightly cover with lids and store in refrigerator until ready to use.

YIELD: 2 pints

BONUS: If you should have an old-style "clamp-on lid jar," fill one and give to your best friend—she will become an even greater friend.

SPICED APPLE CIDER

Hot apple cider is reserved for the chill of Fall and cold of Winter. Many creations abound, but the bunnies and I trust that you will fancy the likes of this special cider.

8 cups apple cider or apple juice	1 teaspoon whole allspice
1/2 cup light brown sugar	16 whole cloves
4 cinnamon sticks	1 medium orange, sliced thin

In a large saucepan, mix together the cider and brown sugar.

In a square of double-thick cotton cheesecloth, place the cinnamon sticks, allspice and cloves. Bring up corners of the cheesecloth and tie with string.

Add the spices and orange slices to cider, bring to boiling; reduce the heat and simmer covered for about 10 minutes.

With slotted spoon, remove spice bag and orange slices. If desired, extra orange slices can be served with the hot cider.

BONUS: Make ahead and store in refrigerator. To reheat you can use microwave.

YIELD: 8 - 10 servings

CAFÉ AU LAIT MIX

This special flavored coffee mix makes great festive gifts for anyone, anytime of the year. Purchase a unique cup, fill it with the mix, wrap in cellophane and ribbon and give it to a best friend as a "just because" gesture. Put a note on the cup with directions on concocting the drink.

2 cups powdered nonfat
   dry milk
1/2 cup instant coffee
   powder

1/2 cup powdered sugar
1/2 teaspoon cinnamon,
   cloves and freshly ground
   nutmeg

Mix all ingredients until well blended and store in an airtight container.

BONUS: Double or triple the recipe so you can make up several "gift cups."

To serve: spoon 1/4 cup of the café au lait mix into a mug and add 2/3 cup boiling water. Serve with a chocolate spoon and add a splotch of whipped cream on top. Yummmmmmmmmmmm!

BONUS: To make an extra-wonderful gift, use instant espresso coffee powder in place of just regular instant coffee powder.

YIELD: 2 cups mix

❦

SUGARED GRAPES (A GARNISH)

Many times you will read a recipe that calls for sugared grapes as a garnish and then neglect to tell you how to make them. Here is a simple method. Enjoy showing off the next time you find it essential to add a hint of glamour to your buffet table.

2 cups granulated sugar	1 bunch grapes, cut into
2 egg whites	clusters

BE SURE GRAPES ARE DRY BEFORE SUGARING

Place sugar in medium bowl. Beat whites in another medium bowl until just frothy.

Dip grape clusters into whites. Shake off excess and toss the clusters in sugar, coating completely.

Transfer to a rack for drying.

BONUS: You can use red or green seedless grapes. Pick out the biggest grapes for nicest clusters.

❦

STYLISH CRANBERRY CHUTNEY

Definitely in style, Cranberry Chutney is a superb holiday house gift. Prepare it as soon as fresh cranberries show up at the market.

4 cups whole fresh
  cranberries
2-1/2 cups granulated sugar
1 cup water
6 whole cloves
2 cinnamon sticks
1/2 teaspoon salt
1 cup light raisins
2 tart apples peeled, cored
  and diced

2 firm pears, peeled, cored
  and diced
1 small onion, chopped
1/2 cup sliced celery
1/2 cup chopped toasted
  walnuts
1 teaspoon grated lemon
  zest

Combine the first 6 ingredients in a large, deep saucepan and blend well. Bring to boil stirring frequently. Cook about 10 minutes or until cranberries start to "pop." Add the raisins, apples, pears, onion and celery. Continue cooking, stirring frequently until thick. This should take about 15 minutes.

Remove from heat and stir in the toasted walnuts and zest. Ladle into sterilized jars and process in boiling water bath according to instructions that come with the jars.

BONUS: You should yield 2 quarts. I like to use pint jars which will double the take. The smaller jars make nicer gifts.

P.S. Spread walnuts on cookie sheet and toast at 275 degrees - shake pan and watch that they don't burn. Check at 5 minutes and often thereafter if they aren't toasted in that time span.

❧

CHOCOLATE WAFFLE COOKIE

A novel means of fashioning a waffle. A plate of these cookies will put a sparkle in everyone's eyes. Great for a May Day festivity. Surprise a friend with a May basket of these cheerful morsels. (Don't forget to ring the doorbell and run).

You will need a waffle iron for making these friendly cookies.

3 squares semi-sweet chocolate	1-1/2 cups granulated sugar
1 cup margarine	2 cups all purpose flour
4 eggs	1 teaspoon vanilla extract
	Dash of salt

Melt the chocolate squares and margarine over medium heat. Remove from heat and cool.

In a medium bowl, beat the eggs; add the chocolate mixture and sugar. Add vanilla and gradually stir in the flour and salt.

Spoon batter into each section of the waffle iron and cook one minute.

Remove waffle cookies; cool on wire rack.

Frost with frosting of your choice.

If you don't have a round waffle iron, you can cut the waffle sections into desired shapes.

TOASTY PUMPKIN SEEDS

Excellent snack material. Also tasty with a pre-dinner cocktail! (Do they still call them cocktails or is this another one of those words that is dating me?) Oh, well...

PREHEAT OVEN: 250 degrees F.

2 cups pumpkin seeds, shells left on, fibers rubbed off (DO NOT WASH)	1 tablespoon peanut oil 1 tablespoon butter 1-1/2 teaspoons kosher or any other coarse salt

Combine all ingredients in a small bowl. Mix well. Spread out on baking sheet or other shallow pan; toast, stirring often, 30-40 minutes or until the seeds are evenly browned and crispy.

Cool and store in tightly covered containers.

REMOVE SHELLS BEFORE EATING.

RHUBARB & ONION RELISH

Everyone is always looking for innovative ways to use rhubarb. This is an attractive, delicious relish. If you have frozen a supply of rhubarb, you can make this unusual recipe for Christmas hostess gifts.

4 cups chopped rhubarb
4 cups chopped white
  onions
2 cups (1 pint) cider
  vinegar
1 tablespoon salt
4 cups brown sugar

1 teaspoon each cloves,
  allspice and cinnamon
Cayenne to taste—
(up to 1 teaspoon for a
hot relish)

Combine all ingredients and cook slowly until thickened. Pour while still hot into hot, sterilized canning jars and seal immediately according to manufacturer's instructions.

BONUS: Exceptionally tasty!

YIELD: 6 to 8 cups

McGEE'S RASPBERRY GLAZE

...and I don't mean "Fibber McGee"... McGee's raspberry glaze is especially yummy used on Rock Cornish Game Hens, but will do equally as well on whatever else needs a refreshing twist.

1 10-ounce package frozen raspberries, thawed but not drained
1/2 cup good red currant jelly

3 teaspoons cornstarch
1 tablespoon cold water

Mix the cornstarch and cold water together to use as the thickener.

In a medium saucepan, bring the raspberries and jelly to a hard boil and stir in the cornstarch/water mix. Remove from heat and cool.

Store in refrigerator until used for glazing. The glaze is particularly wonderful on baked pheasant for those of us auspicious enough to have some on hand.

❧

COOKIE BAR POPS

A remarkable treat that's fun for the whole family to build. Use up a snowy or rainy day to put these treats together. You'll have a stupendous time.

PREHEAT OVEN: 375 degrees F.

1/2 cup brown sugar, packed firmly
1/2 cup granulated sugar
1/2 cup butter or margarine, softened
1/2 cup smooth peanut butter
1 teaspoon vanilla extract
1 large egg

1-1/2 cups all purpose flour
1/2 teaspoon baking powder
1/2 teaspoon baking soda
1/4 teaspoon salt

10 wooden popsicle sticks
10 fun-size candy bars such as Milky Way® or Snickers®

In a large mixer bowl mix together the brown sugar, granulated sugar, butter or margarine, peanut butter, vanilla extract and egg; beat well.

Add flour, baking powder, baking soda and salt. Mix well.

Insert the sticks into narrow end of the candy bars and make sure they are securely "fastened." Mold about 1/3 cup of cookie dough smoothly around each candy bar, making sure that the bar is completely surrounded.

Recipe Continues...

COOKIE BAR POPS

Continued...

Place the candy bar pops 4 inches apart on ungreased cookie sheets. Bake about 15 minutes or until cookies are lightly browned. Remove from oven, cool 10 minutes; remove from cookie sheets and cool completely.

BONUS: These cookies are delightfully easy to make. I found wooden sticks at the local craft store. Also you can find them at a baker's or candy maker's supply store.

YIELD: 10 cookie bar pops

ESKIMO COOKIES

Befitting their title, these fun to make and good to eat cookies are unbaked and are at home in the refrigerator. The kids on your block will unquestionably fancy these treats not only for eating but for creating. Pam says that even the youngest children can roll the cookies in the confectioner's sugar. Another "festive occasion" looms in your future.

3/4 cup butter
3/4 cup granulated sugar
1 tablespoon water
1/2 teaspoon vanilla extract

3 tablespoons cocoa
2 cups instant oatmeal
flakes

Cream the butter and sugar, add water, vanilla and cocoa. Stir in oatmeal. Chill well (best if held overnight in an igloo.) Shape into small balls and roll in confectioner's sugar. Store in refrigerator.

160

GIANT CHOCOLATE SANDWICH COOKIES

For the KIDS or "KIDS AT HEART." Have you heard of "queen for a day." Well, this giant cookie should be called "cookie for a week." One of these cookies will feed the "Green Giant" for one day but will keep the "kids" happy for lunch every day of the week. A great weekend project for the bored members of your household. However, no one will know if you sneak a few minutes out of your busy schedule to have some fun, too.

PREHEAT OVEN: 350 degrees F.

COOKIE:

1 6-ounce package chocolate morsels	1/4 teaspoon salt
1-3/4 cups all purpose flour	2/3 cup shortening
2 teaspoons baking soda	2/3 cup granulated sugar
1 teaspoon ground cinnamon	1 egg
	1/4 cup light corn syrup

Melt the chocolate morsels; set aside.

In a small bowl, combine the flour, soda, cinnamon, and salt.

Recipe Continues...

161

GIANT CHOCOLATE SANDWICH COOKIES
Continued...

In a large mixer bowl, place the shortening, 2/3 cup sugar and egg. Beat until creamy. Add the corn syrup and melted chocolate. Blend in the flour mixture.

Divide the dough into two parts. Roll out each part into a large circle like you would a pizza. Bake on pizza pan or large cookie sheet for 25 minutes at 350 degrees F.

FILLING:

1 tablespoon butter, softened
1/4 teaspoon peppermint extract

2 cups powdered sugar
2 to 3 tablespoons milk.

While cookies are baking, mix the filling and set aside.

After the two cookies are cool, frost one of them with the filling and stack the other on top like an Oreo cookie.

CHEERFUL ZOO MIX

Another happy project for the kids in your life whether they be 6 or 60. This mid-day treat is a show stopper that will substitute for those rainy days at the playground. This is a quick and easy indoor venture.

Mix together the following cereals and other snacks:

2 cups Apple Cinnamon Cheerios cereal
2 cups plain Cheerios cereal
2 cups honey nut Cheerios cereal

1-1/2 cups animal crackers of your choice

2 cups miniature pretzel twists

1-1/2 cups any cheese-flavored snack crackers

1/2 package 5.4 ounce size of The Berry Bears, Shark Bites, Surf's Up or Thunder Jets chewy fruit snack

In a big bowl mix all of cereals and crackers, etc.
Store in an airtight container.

MAKES ABOUT 10-1/2 cups of your favorite snack.

BEST MAN'S FAVORITE SALSA

Absolutely the best ever salsa and named after the "best" man at our wedding who is sharing his salsa with us. Best prepared with fresh garden tomatoes but most certainly can be formulated with tomatoes any time of the year.

1 pound white onions chopped
1/2 pound jalepeños or one 11-1/2-ounce jar with liquid
2 small green chilies—fresh is best but you can use canned
(2 small cans chopped and seeded)
10 pounds to 13 pounds fresh ripe tomatoes chopped

1 tablespoon salt
1/2 tablespoon pepper
1 clove garlic minced
1/2 cup vinegar (Best of Friends raspberry vinegar is great)
1/4 cup granulated sugar
2 or 3 small cans tomato paste
1 package taco seasoning mix—your choice

In a large kettle, mix all ingredients and bring to boil (about 15 minutes).

Pack in various size canning jars and hot bath process for 20 minutes.

BONUS: If the salsa needs a little more liquid use tomato juice. Also—adjust the seasonings. This recipe is medium "hot." Some people prefer a little more "fire" with their salsa—have at it!

YIELD: About 14 pint jars

EFFORTLESS
ASPARAGUS PICKLES

Easy to prepare, these pickled asparagus are fun to have on hand year round. Use with Bloody Marys instead of celery sticks or for a basic healthy snack.

4 pounds very thin green asparagus
2 onions sliced very thin
2 red bell peppers, cut in julienne strips, seeds removed

2 teaspoons salt
5 cups cider vinegar
3 tablespoons sugar
3 tablespoons mixed pickling spices
2 cups water

Wash the asparagus thoroughly in cold water. Lay the onions neatly on the bottoms of two 1-quart jars. Pack the asparagus cut ends down with the red pepper strips to give a striped effect to the filled jars.

Boil the remaining ingredients for 10 minutes. Fill jars with hot mixture. Seal and process for 20 minutes.

YIELD: 2 quarts

MEXICAN SAUSAGE/ CHEESE BITES!

"Some like it hotter than others." These snappy little sausage/cheese combinations can make one's eyes water in a second. However, if you are a lover of spicy-hot, don't put off making these sausage and cheese bites.

1 pound Mexican Cheese such as Velveeta®–room temperature
1 pound lean ground sausage

2 cups biscuit mix such as Bisquick®

Mix together in a large bowl the room temperature cheese, sausage and biscuit mix–using your hands works perfectly. Form into teaspoon size balls and bake on cookie sheet at 350 degrees F. for 18 to 20 minutes.

Serve hot out of the oven.

BONUS: You can use spicy hot sausage along with the Mexican cheese if your physical being can handle it. These "bites" can also be reheated.

YIELD: 40-50 sausage/cheese balls

CANDIED CITRUS PEEL

Garnish with "a peel" using the microwave to assist in making candied citrus peel for those eye-catching desserts. Using candied peels is like adding frosting to a cake. Have fun!

2 large oranges	1 cup granulated sugar,
4 lemons	divided in half
4 limes, or	3 tablespoons water
1 large grapefruit	

Work over a small bowl to catch the juice from one of the above fruits of your choice. Remove the peel from that fruit with a sharp paring knife.

Cut the pith (the white underpart of the peel) away from the peel and cut peeling into very narrow strips (about 1/8-inch wide).

Combine 1/2 cup of the sugar and water in a 1-quart microwavable casserole; microwave at HIGH 1-1/2 minutes. Stir in the peel and microwave at HIGH 6 to 8 minutes, stirring every 2 minutes, or until peel tests tender.

Recipe Continues...

CANDIED CITRUS PEEL
Continued...

Place the remaining 1/2 cup granulated sugar in a pie plate. Remove fruit peel from casserole with slotted spoon; drain well on paper toweling. Add peel to pipe plate of sugar in batches and toss until well coated. Place the sugared peel on waxed paper and allow to dry—about an hour. Store in an airtight container.

BONUS: Make an extra batch of peel to use for a hostess gift. Add peel to a fresh spinach salad, sprinkle on baked ham the last 10 minutes of baking, or mince the peel and stir into a sugar cookie dough before baking.

YIELD: 1-1/2 cups

CHOCOLATE DIP
STRAWBERRIES

A favorite with the Easter Brunch Crowd. This is usually my contribution to the brunch. Everyone thinks they are hard to do, but believe me, they aren't. Have fun dipping!

About 36 large fresh
  strawberries

1/4 bar paraffin

12-ounce bag semisweet
  chocolate baking chips

Rinse strawberries. Do not remove stems. Drain and dry. The strawberries must be dry in order for the melted chocolate to adhere to them.

In a double boiler, melt the chocolate chips and paraffin together. Hang on to the stem of the berry and dip into the melted chocolate mixture. Drain on a waxed paper lined cookie sheet. Let the berries dry. They are best if served the same day you dip them. They can be refrigerated until serving time, but they do not hold up well if done the night before. I usually get up early Easter morning and do them before "church." They are ready and rarin' to go by noon. USE YOUR OWN JUDGMENT ON THE TIME.

BONUS: The paraffin can be found with the "jelly canning supplies." If you can't find stemmed strawberries, use a toothpick to dip them.

MACADAMIA CHIP COOKIES

I'm always looking for something new and different in the chocolate chip cookie world. This macadamia nut, chocolate chip combination is divinely decadent!

PREHEAT OVEN: 325 degrees F.

1 cup softened sweet butter
3/4 cup granulated sugar
3/4 cup firmly packed
  brown sugar
1 tablespoon vanilla extract
1 tablespoon Frangelico
  liqueur (optional)
1 tablespoon coffee liqueur
2 large eggs

2-1/2 cups all purpose flour
1 teaspoon baking soda
1/4 teaspoon salt
2 12-ounce packages milk
  chocolate chips
1 cup chopped walnuts
1/2 cup chopped pecans
1/2 cup chopped macadamia
  nuts

Using large mixer bowl, cream first 6 ingredients until light and fluffy. Add the eggs and beat well. Mix flour, baking soda and salt in bowl. Stir into the creamed mixture. Mix in chocolate chips and all chopped nuts by hand. Drop batter by 1/4 cupfuls onto greased cookie sheets. Space cookies about 1-inch apart. Bake until cookies are light brown, about 15 minutes. Remove from oven and transfer to wire racks. Cool completely.

BONUS: Cookies can be eaten warm from the oven, but be careful not to burn your mouth.

YIELD: Makes about 36 cookies

BAKED SANDWICH GOOTCH

Significantly unlike any sandwich I have ever tasted, this made-in-a-bowl, make-ahead sandwich could become habit forming. Try it for Sunday A.M. brunch. Father's Day would be perfect timing to impress the Dad in your house.

4 slices French bread
2 slices Swiss cheese
2 slices cooked ham
2 eggs

1/4 cup dry white wine such
  as chablis
1 cup 2% milk
1/2 teaspoon salt

For each sandwich, butter the outside of two slices of bread. Place ham and cheese slices between. Place each "sandwich" in pottery bowls.

Beat eggs, add milk, wine and salt. Pour over the sandwiches. Let stand 1 hour or overnight.

Remove from refrigerator and bake in 350 degree F. oven for about 55 minutes.

Serve with Caesar salad and white wine.

BONUS: Double recipe to make more sandwiches.

SWEET AND SOUR DIPPING

Extremely delightful—this apricot flavored dipping sauce is just perfect for those Wanton appetizers you have stashed away in your freezer. If, however, the cupboard is bare, purchase a supply from your favorite "Chinese Cookery" and don't tell anyone that you didn't prepare them yourself. The dipping sauce is good enough to make everyone think you made the Wontons, too.

2/3 cup apricot-pineapple preserves or 1/3 cup of each	1 tablespoon white vinegar
	1/8 teaspoon Tabasco® flavoring sauce
2 tablespoons water	Pinch of minced garlic or
1 tablespoon catsup	garlic juice

Combine all ingredients in saucepan. Heat just to boiling, stirring occasionally.

Serve warm as dipping sauce for Wonton appeteasers.

BONUS: If you have never used garlic juice, you can find it in the spice section at most super markets. It is easier to use in most recipes that call for garlic and equally mixes in with any recipe asking for garlic.

YIELD: 3/4 cup

BAKED APPLE BUTTER

This recipe for apple butter is basic and simple. I recommend it highly. It is, in my opinion, the only method for using up that overload of backyard apples.

4 to 5 pounds—about 12 large—cooking apples 3 cups cider or apple juice Brown sugar	Cinnamon, cloves, allspice and freshly ground nutmeg to taste (See following instructions)

Wash and quarter apples; remove stems and any blemishes. Place in a large pan and add the apple juice or cider. Cover and cook the apples until quite soft. Remove from heat, drain and force fruit through a colander or food mill; measure the pulp.

For every cup of fruit pulp, stir in about 1/2 cup brown sugar, depending upon the sweetness of the apples and spices to taste. I use about 2 teaspoons cinnamon, 1/2 teaspoon cloves, 1 teaspoon allspice and 1/4 teaspoon nutmeg with 4 to 5 pounds apples. You can add or detract to satisfy your taste.

Place fruit in a heavy banking pan and bake in a 275 degree F. oven until the butter becomes thick and dark.

Pour hot into sterilized jelly jars and seal according to manufacturer's directions for hot-bath sealing jars.

BONUS: If you wish, the apple butter may be partially cooked on top of stove and then placed in oven. I prefer baking it.

YIELD: 9 cups

FOCACCIA BREAD

Focaccia (foh-CAH-chee-ah) is akin to pizza but cut into small wedges or squares, it is a perfect tag-along to soups or salads. We like to serve it as an appeteaser. Focaccia is also a great accompaniment to spaghetti. This recipe is geared to a bread machine.

1 cup water
3 tablespoons extra virgin
  olive oil
1/2 cup vegetable oil

1/2 teaspoon salt
1/3 teaspoons basil or
  rosemary
1 tablespoon sugar
4-1/2 cups bread flour
2 teaspoons yeast

Following directions for your particular bread machine, prepare the dough. Remove from machine and using your fingers, press dough onto a lightly greased pizza pan or any other baking sheet. Cover and let rise for about one-half hour. Spread topping over the dough and bake in a preheated 375 degree F. oven for about 30 minutes—watch carefully so as not to over bake.

1/4 teaspoon garlic powder
  (optional)
1/4 cup extra virgin olive oil
1/2 teaspoon basil leaves,
  crushed

1/2 teaspoon fennel
2 teaspoons sea salt
  (optional)

Recipe Continues...

174

FOCACCIA BREAD
Continued...

Mix the topping ingredients together in a small bowl before spreading over the Focaccia.

BONUS: If you don't have a bread machine, prepare the dough "by hand" as you would for any bread dough.

YIELD: This recipe will make 2 large "breads"

—NOTES—

POTABLES:

HOLIDAYS FANTASTIC

POTABLES
Index

SYLLABUB

A centuries-old beverage, Syllabub is one of many traditional Christmas drinks. Syllabub originated in "merry old England" and is still a part of festive celebrations. Special cups are used to serve this special "brew" but demitasse cups or a special holiday mug can certainly be substituted.

1 quart whipping cream	3/4 cup granulated sugar
1-1/2 cups milk (2% or skim)	1 teaspoon vanilla extract
2/3 cup sweet Sauternes or other sweet white wine	Freshly grated nutmeg

In a large mixing bowl or punch bowl, beat at medium speed with electric mixer until frothy all ingredients except the nutmeg.

Pour immediately into chilled cups and dust with freshly grated nutmeg. Enjoy!

YIELD: 8 servings

MERRY MOCHA NOG

Especially developed for those of us who enjoy chocolate more than any other flavor. Those of you who can take it or leave it will smack your lips and lick your fingers after you have the opportunity to join in the merriment of this chocolate "tasting bee."

2/3 **cup instant espresso**
2/3 **cup sugar**
2/3 **cup water**
1/3 **cup instant chocolate mix such as Nestle's**

1 **pint (or more) vanilla ice cream**
2 **quarts cold skim milk**
1 **quart chocolate ice cream**

Mix together the espresso coffee, sugar, water and instant chocolate and blend well. Beat in the vanilla ice cream which has been allowed to soften. Blend in milk.

Pour into a punch bowl and spoon chocolate ice cream over all.

BONUS: Creme de cacao or Kahlua to taste may be added or you can make one recipe with the liqueur and one without.

Also you can use regular instant coffee in place of the instant espresso.

EGGNOG RENEWED

Eggnog is traditionally served cold. This updated version is served hot and spicy. I suggest you not ponder too long before experiencing this delightful innovation.

EGGNOG MIX—ENOUGH TO SERVE 30 GUESTS

6 large egg yolks	1/4 teaspoon cream of tartar
3/4 cup water	2 pounds sifted
6 egg whites	confectioners sugar

Combine the egg yolks and water in a medium saucepan. Cook and stir over medium heat for 5 to 6 minutes or until mixture thickens and coats the back of a metal spoon. Remove from heat and cover with plastic wrap. Cool mixture.

Beat egg whites and cream of tartar until stiff peaks form—do not overbeat.

As soon as egg yolk mixture has cooled, fold into the beaten egg whites. Next, gradually beat in one-half of the sifted confectioners sugar.

Cover mix and freeze until serving guests. Any leftover mix should be frozen.

Recipe Continues...

EGGNOG RENEWED

Continued...

TO SERVE:

For each GUEST you will need:

3/4 **cup boiling water in a heat proof mug or cup**

1 **tablespoon brandy or brandy flavoring**

1 **tablespoon rum or rum flavoring**

1/4 **cup eggnog mix**

Generous "grind" of fresh nutmeg (pre-ground is acceptable) on top of eggnog.

HAPPY HOLIDAYS!

❧

182

CHRISTMAS TREE PUNCH

This beautiful green punch is just the right touch for Christmas Eve entertaining.

1 6-ounce can frozen
lemonade concentrate,
thawed
2 6-ounce cans frozen
limeade concentrate,
thawed

2 cups water
2 28-ounce bottles gingerale
Green food coloring
Ice or ice mold

In a glass punch bowl or very large non-metal pitcher, combine all concentrates and water. Stir in desired amount of food coloring. Chill. Just before serving, add the ginerale and ice, stirring to blend.

BONUS: An ice ring with red and green cherries would complete this special holiday punch.

YIELD: 20 half-cup servings

NOEL BOWL

This Christmas punch brings out the best in all of us. It can be served with or without alcohol or you can make a bowl of each. Also, depending where you are during the holiday season, you can serve it warmed or over ice—you be the judge and jury!

4 cups water	8 cups apple cider or
2 cups granulated sugar	apple juice
12 cloves (whole)	3 cups orange juice—fresh
6 cinnamon sticks	is best
6 allspice berries	2 cups fresh lemon juice
1 tablespoon fresh ginger	(about 8 lemons
chopped (where available)	depending on size)
	rum (optional)

In a large saucepan, mix the first six ingredients, bring to a boil and stir to dissolve the sugar. Simmer for 10 minutes.

Remove the syrup from heat, cover and let stand 1 hour.

Pour the syrup through a strainer into a large bowl. Stir in the juices, cover and refrigerate until serving.

BONUS: Punch can be prepared two days ahead of party. Serve cold or heat gently just before serving. Your guests can add their own rum if desired. Set out both dark and light rum for a choice.

YIELD: 12 servings

CHRISTMAS WASSAIL

Christmas would not be Christmas without serving a Wassail Bowl.

2 quarts apple cider
1/2 cup brown sugar
1/3 cup frozen lemon juice
  concentrate, thawed
1/3 cup frozen orange juice
  concentrate, thawed

6 cinnamon sticks
3 whole cloves
3 whole allspice
1/2 teaspoon freshly grated
  nutmeg
2 "Fifths" good dry sherry

Combine the cider, brown sugar and fruit concentrates in a kettle. Add the cinnamon, cloves, allspice and nutmeg. Bring to boiling; cover and simmer 20 minutes.

Remove the whole spices. Add sherry and heat again just to boiling.

BONUS: Serve hot in small mugs or special dessert cups. A bowl of warm spicy nuts would be a delight!

LEMON VODKA

Flavored vodkas are "in." They make fun holiday gifts and they are useable in making special festive drinks for various festivals throughout the year. Fancy bottles are available for "gift wrapping."

4 lemons
1 quart good vodka

Using a citrus stripper, or sharp paring knife, remove lemon rinds in long, thin strips. Do not use the white pith as it is bitter. Add the lemon rind to the bottle of vodka and place it in the freezer for at least 3 days, shaking it whenever you get the urge.

You can store the vodka in the freezer until you are ready to deliver it to a friend. I am told vodka from the freezer is the only way to go!

BONUS: Hot Pepper Vodka is excellent used for "Bloody Marys." To give as a Christmas gift, I add one long red pepper and one long hot green pepper to a quart of vodka. It, too, can be stored in the freezer or refrigerator. WARNING!!! The longer it is stored, the hotter it gets.

NEW YEAR'S BRUNCH PUNCH

We all need an eye-opener after the holidays and New Year's is certainly no exception to the rule. This delicious "bubbly" drink qualifies for the "eye-opener" of the day.

4 cups cranberry juice
  cocktail
1 cup water
1/2 of a 6-ounce can orange
  juice concentrate (1/3 cup)

6 cinnamon sticks
1 750 MM bottle
  champagne, chilled

Combine the cranberry juice cocktail, water, orange juice concentrate and cinnamon sticks in a large saucepan. Bring to boiling uncovered and simmer for 5 minutes. Strain, cover and chill.

Just before serving pour the cranberry mixture into a small punch bowl or an impressive crystal pitcher, gradually pouring the champagne down the side of the bowl or pitcher. Stir very "softly."

BONUS: Cool this sparkling punch with ice cubes studded with slices of orange and cranberries. To make ice cubes, cut orange slices to fit into compartments of an ice cube tray. Add a few raw cranberries to each; fill with water and freeze.

YIELD: 18 one-half cup servings

APPETEASERS:

APPETEASERS
Index

GLORIOUS BRANDIED CRANBERRIES

No words can express the greatness of these brandied cranberries. Delicious and versatile all year long.

4 cups fresh cranberries   1/3 cup blackberry brandy
2 cups granulated sugar

Wash and clean the cranberries

Place the cranberries in a 9 x 13-inch cake pan. Sprinkle evenly with the 2 cups of sugar. Cover with foil and bake at 300 degrees F. for 1 hour.

Carefully stir in the blackberry brandy. Store in refrigerator in sealed jars or use the hot water bath method per canning jar directions for sealing the cranberries for a longer shelf life.

BONUS: The brandied cranberries can be used as a sauce, warmed and served with ham, over warmed Brie cheese for an appeteaser, as an ice cream topping and as an accompaniment to your Thanksgiving turkey. There is no end to its versatility.

P.S. Frozen cranberries can be used if you get desperate. Fresh, however, are better.

YIELD: 3-4 cups

ENJOY!!!!!

KAY'S FAVORITE BLUE CHEESE CAKE, AN APPETEASER!

If you are a blue cheese fanatic this absolutely savory appetizer is a must for your next special event—even if it may just be a TGIF celebration.
Try it now!

PREHEAT OVEN: 325 degrees F.

2 tablespoons butter
1 cup crushed cheese
  crackers
16 ounces low fat cream
  cheese
8 ounces blue cheese
3 eggs

1/4 cup flour
1/4 teaspoon salt
1/4 cup picante sauce
1 cup dairy sour cream
1/2 cup chopped green
  onions
1/2 cup finely chopped
  pecans

Butter an 8-inch spring form pan.
Sprinkle cracker crumbs on bottom and up sides of pan.

Blend together the cheeses, eggs, flour, salt, sour cream, and picante sauce. Stir in the onions.

Recipe Continues...

192

KAY'S FAVORITE BLUE CHEESE CAKE, AN APPETEASER!

Continued...

Pour batter into pan, sprinkle the chopped pecans on top and bake for 1 hour. Remove from oven, cool, and then refrigerate.

Serve cheesecake at room temperature with your favorite crackers.

BONUS: If you have any leftover cheesecake, cut several wedges, wrap each wedge in plastic wrap and then place in a plastic bag. Freeze for another celebration or send a wedge home with your dinner guests.

🍒

SPECIALIZED
UBIQUITOUS CRAB

What started out to be an appeteaser ended up being "ubiquitous." You will find that a can or two of crab will lead you and your friends into oblivion no matter what you choose to create. My very favorite are the crab cup appeteasers as follows:

2 - 8 oz. packages low fat
    cream cheese, softened
3/4 cup low fat mayonnaise
1/2 cup sharp cheddar
    cheese, grated
1 or 2-6 oz. cans "fancy
    lump" crabmeat

6 green onions minced
2 eggs—hard cooked and
    diced
1/2 teaspoon paprika
1/4 teaspoon dry mustard
Dash or two of freshly
    ground pepper

Mix the cream cheese with the mayonnaise.
Add remaining ingredients and mix well. Refrigerate until served.

Serve as an appeteaser with biscuits, crackers, rye thins, etc.

BONUS: My favorite way to serve the ubiquitous crab is to create mini pie shells by using refrigerated pie dough and using a fluted cookie cutter (7 inches in circumference and 2 inches deep) and mini-muffin pan. The muffin pan should have deep cups. Do not use the pans that have very shallow cups—they are used for tarts etc.

Recipe Continues...

SPECIALIZED UBIQUITOUS CRAB
Continued...

Follow directions on package for making the shells. Fill the cooled shells with the crab mixture which can be served cold or heated.

YIELD: I usually get at least 36 mini shells from the recipe. You can get more or less depending on what you do with crabmeat mixture.

SOME OTHER VARIETIES:

1. Combine well with rice or noodles for a casserole. Increase mayonnaise and bake at 350 degrees F. for 40 minutes.

2. Add chopped celery and/or green and red pepper for a delicious holiday crab salad.

3. Can be served from a chafing dish as a crab spread for crackers or bread.

4. Makes marvelous crab sandwiches—just add a little mayonnaise so that it spreads nicely.

CHOCOLATE POPCORN BALLS

Miriam says "Serve these anywhere to the young 6 - 60! A hit at my cocktail party."

3/4 cup granulated sugar
1/4 cup white corn syrup
1/2 cup water
Pinch of salt

1-1/2 quarts (6 cups) popped corn (Keep warm in oven)
1-1/2 squares (1-1/2 ounces) bitter baking chocolate
1-1/2 tablespoons butter

Dissolve sugar, syrup, water and pinch of salt in saucepan over low heat; then cook (medium high heat) to 242 degrees F. on candy thermometer or medium firm ball stage in cold water. Melt butter and chocolate in separate saucepan and add quickly to the cooked syrup mixture at this point. Stir together and pour over warm popcorn. Stir to mix and form into 12 balls.

BONUS: I made the popcorn balls smaller and served them at a Christmas brunch. Miriam—you are right. Smaller size would definitely be prodigious conversation during cocktails!

YIELD: 12 popcorn balls

196

OPEN HOUSE
CHOCOLATE CHEESE

This chocolate cheese is a special treat. It truly melts in one's mouth. Definitely unique in texture and taste. Construct this beautiful chocolate Cheese soon.

8 ounces low fat cream cheese	1/4 cup granulated sugar
4 squares German chocolate, melted	1 egg yolk
	1 teaspoon Hershey cocoa

Combine all ingredients in a food processor or blender until smooth. Shape or mold as desired. Decorate with chocolate curls or sprinkles. Refrigerate before serving.

BONUS: Sherry says that the measurements are approximate and one must taste to do it right. In any event, the chocolate cheese is great served with shortbread or sugar cookies.

197

HOLIDAY PEPPER RELISH

A colorful pepper relish designed to be consumed as an appeteaser. This is definitely for all of us people-on-the go!

2 green bell peppers
2 red bell peppers
2 yellow bell peppers
1 lime juiced
1 tablespoon chopped
   cilantro

1 tablespoon red wine
   vinegar or "Best of
   Friends" raspberry
   vinegar

Chop peppers into 1/4 inch pieces. Squeeze the lime juice over the peppers; add cilantro, oil and vinegar. Toss lightly.

Chill for at least 2 hours.

Serve with tortilla chips.

SALMON PHYLLO PACKETS

An easy but delectable appeteaser appropriate for any festive event. Phyllo pastry dough is fun to work with and becomes the centerpiece of attention whenever it is served.

1 6-3/4 oz. can red salmon, drained and flaked. (Don't pinch your pennies when buying salmon—buy the best.)

1/2 cup thawed and drained frozen sweet peas

1 2 oz. jar pimiento, drained and diced

1/2 cup shredded Swiss cheese

6 frozen phyllo sheets, thawed—each sheet 18 x 14 inches

1/4 cup margarine or butter, melted

Dill weed

PREHEAT OVEN: 350 degrees F.
Ungreased cookie sheets

In a medium mixing bowl, combine the drained salmon, peas, pimiento and cheese.

Unroll phyllo sheets; cover with plastic wrap or damp towel.

Carefully place one phyllo sheet on work area; brush with melted margarine; continue layering with 2 more phyllo sheets, brushing each with the melted margarine.

Recipe Continues...

SALMON PHYLLO PACKETS
Continued...

With a very sharp knife, cut through all layers of the phyllo dough creating 20 rectangles.

Place a heaping teaspoonful of the salmon mixture in center of each phyllo rectangle and shape into packet by folding all sides around the salmon filling forming packet. Place folded side down on ungreased cookie sheets. Sprinkle with dill weed and bake at 350 degrees F. 18 to 20 minutes or until lightly browned.

REPEAT with remaining 3 Phyllo sheets.

BONUS: Appeteasers can also be shaped into little sacks by placing a heaping teaspoonful of salmon mixture in center of each rectangle. Bring up edges of the pastry and twist together with circular motion.

Can be made 24 hours before you need. Cover and refrigerate until ready to bake.

P.S. Phyllo dough can be found in the freezer compartments of most super markets. Thaw before using.

❧

BRIE AND WALNUTS

An easy appetizer full of surprises. Particularly ideal for Holiday festivities.

1 4-1/2 ounce round Brie cheese
2 tablespoons crumbled blue cheese
3 tablespoons chopped walnuts

2 sheets frozen phyllo dough thawed and halved crosswise
2 tablespoons melted margarine or butter

Slice the Brie in half horizontally. Sprinkle the crumbled blue cheese and 2 tablespoons of the chopped walnuts over the cut side of bottom half. Replace the top half of Brie.

Brush 1 half-sheet of the phyllo with melted margarine; place the Brie in center of the buttered phyllo sheet. Cover remaining phyllo dough with a damp cloth to keep from drying out.

Wrap the buttered phyllo around Brie. Turn cheese over. Repeat the brushing and wrapping with the remaining half-sheets of phyllo, turning cheese over after wrapping with each half-sheet.

Recipe Continues...

BRIE AND WALNUTS

Continued...

Brush wrapped cheese with melted margarine and sprinkle with remaining chopped walnuts. At this point bake, or cover and chill.

For baking, place the completed Brie in a shallow baking pan. Bake at 425 degrees F. for 10 minutes or until just golden. Let the Brie cool just a bit before slicing.

BONUS: Brie is delicious served with Granny Smith apple wedges. You can make the Brie early in the day and keep chilled in refrigerator until baking. Make one for yourself and give the other to a best friend. I have on occasion prepared two cheese rounds and frozen one of them.

SAUCY SANDWICH SPREAD

Unconventional in its ingredients, this sauce performs prodigiously with sandwiches—especially with beef or turkey.

1 cup low fat mayonnaise
1/3 cup thick, spicy steak
  sauce (your favorite)
3 tablespoons minced fresh
  cilantro or parsley
2 tablespoons minced fresh
  or dried chives
2 tablespoons capers,
  drained

2 tablespoons sweet pickle
  relish, drained
1 tablespoon prepared
  mustard
1/4 to 1/2 teaspoon hot sauce
  (Tabasco)

In a medium bowl, stir all ingredients together, mixing well. Store spread in glass containers in the refrigerator.

BONUS: Fresh cilantro (chinese parsley) is not always available in our local super markets so I usually just use parsley.

This spread is perfect for leftover turkey which needs to be "spruced up a bit" during the holiday aftermath. The recipe also plays doubles nicely.

YIELD: 1-3/4 cups

PROVOLONE CHEESE BREAD

Actually a melted down provolone cheese with herbs and spices make up this appeteaser. Easy on the budget, time spent in the kitchen and readily available ingredients. What else could you ask for?

PREHEAT BROILER

1-1/2 pound round
  provolone cheese
2 teaspoons dried oregano,
  crumbled

1 garlic clove, minced
2 tablespoons extra virgin
  olive oil
Sourdough bread slices

Set cheese in a small broiler-proof baking dish. Sprinkle with oregano and garlic. Drizzle the olive oil over top of cheese.

Broil until cheese melts—which should take about 7 - 8 minutes.

Serve with sourdough bread.

BONUS: Keep a round of provolone on hand for those spur-of-the-moment before dinner snacks. Provolone freezes okay.

YIELD: 4 to 6 first-course servings. Larger yield for appeteaser servings.

SUGAR GLAZED BRIE

Brie is an excellent choice for a festive event of any kind. I like to do brie during the holidays when it is most readily available in the cheese section of bigger super markets. Ask your grocer to order it for you if you don't see it in his store.

1/4 cup packed brown sugar	1 14-ounce round Brie
1/4 cup chopped macadamia	cheese (about 5 inches in
nuts, almonds, pecans or	diameter)
walnuts	Apple wedges, seedless
1 tablespoon brandy	grapes, and crackers
	Lemon juice

In a wide-mouthed canning jar, divide the sugar, nuts and brandy together. Cover; refrigerate up to 1 week. Or transfer the mixture to a moisture and vaporproof freezer container, seal, label and store up to 6 months.

To serve: If frozen, let sugar mixture warm to room temperature for at least 1 hour. Place the cheese on a large round ovenproof platter or 9-inch pie plate. Bake in 500 degree F. oven for 4 to 5 minutes or till cheese is slightly softened. At this point sprinkle sugar mixture over top and bake 2 to 3 minutes or until sugar is melted and the cheese is heated through but do not melt completely.

Recipe Continues...

SUGAR GLAZED BRIE

Continued...

Brush apple slices with lemon juice and arrange with grapes and crackers around cheese.

BONUS: Use two smaller rounds of Brie if you can't locate a 14-inch round.

YIELD: Serves 16 to 20 nicely

BREADS:

BREADS
Index

FAMILY TRADITION LEFSE

Because I have fun making this wonderful family tradition treat, I am sharing a second recipe with you. My friend Judy, her mother and sister have made this part of their traditional Christmas baking marathon. Why not make it part of yours!*!

4 cups cooked, peeled potatoes (half white and half red)	2 tablespoons granulated sugar
1/4 cup butter or margarine	1 teaspoon salt
1/2 cup heavy cream (whipping cream is okay)	1-1/2 cups flour (approximate)

Drain cooked potatoes on paper towel until thoroughly dry. Whip with electric mixer—NOT FOOD PROCESSOR. Beat in the butter, cream, sugar and salt until smooth. Cover and refrigerate overnight. Dough must be cold.

Remove from refrigerator, stir in flour until blended, divide into 20 equal pieces.

Preheat either a lefse griddle or other griddle over medium heat. Roll each ball of dough into a very thin 10-inch circle. Bake about 1 minute on each side until flecked with brown. Stack with wax paper between each. KEEP COVERED, refrigerate or freeze.

Recipe Continues...

FAMILY TRADITION LEFSE

Continued...

BONUS: If the dough handles easily, without sticking or coming apart, you have enough flour in it. If not, you may have to add 1 tablespoon at a time until adjusted correctly.

P.S. Serve warm—spread butter on each "lefse round," sprinkle with cinnamon and sugar, roll up and ENJOY!

P.P.S. If you plan to make more than 20 lefse rounds, I suggest you make another batch of lefse dough rather than doubling the recipe.

P.P.P.S. We like to lightly brown filet of sole in melted butter, squeeze fresh lemon over the sole, roll up in a lightly buttered lefse "pancake" and enjoy as part of our Christmas Eve dinner before attending church services. Serve a fruit salad or whatever fresh fruit is available to you. We like a layered vegetable salad or brandied cranberries with the lefse. A white wine or White-Zinfandel is a pleasant combination. Serve a special dessert after you return from church. Pavlova would be my choice for the specialized dessert, but your own family's favorite would be prodigious.

SIMPLY POPOVERS

These airy, puffy muffins called popovers are appropriately named. They conform to almost any situation and fill that extra little gap where a roll or bread would normally do the trick. Try some for dinner today.

PREHEAT OVEN TO 475 degrees F.

You will need 6 - 8 well-greased custard cups or a popover baking pan.

2 eggs	1/2 teaspoon salt
1 cup milk	1 tablespoon cooking oil
1 cup sifted all purpose flour	

Break the eggs into a mixing bowl. Add milk, flour and salt. Beat 1-1/2 minutes with an electric beater. Add cooking oil and beat 30 seconds, being cautious not to overbeat.

Fill 6 to 8 very-well greased custard cups half full. Bake at 475 degrees F. for 15 minutes. Reduce oven temperature to 350 degrees F. and bake 25 to 30 minutes more. The popovers should be golden brown.

Recipe Continues...

SIMPLY POPOVERS
Continued...

Shortly before removing from oven, prick each popover with a fork to allow the steam to get away. However, if you prefer popovers dry inside, turn off oven; let wait in oven for 20 more minutes, with door ajar. Popovers are tastiest when hot and served with lots of margarine or butter.

BONUS: These can replace Yorkshire Pudding very nicely!

YORKSHIRE PUDDING

Yorkshire pudding is traditionally served with prime rib roast. It is not a pudding but more bread-like. You will need pan drippings to prepare the Yorkshire Pudding, so it necessitates preparation of roast beef.

2 eggs
1 cup milk
1 cup sifted all purpose
  flour

1/2 teaspoon salt
2 tablespoons roast-beef
  drippings

As soon as your roast beef has been removed from the oven, increase the oven temperature to 425 degrees F.

In a medium mixing bowl, with a rotary beater, beat eggs, milk, flour and salt to make a smooth batter.

Pour drippings from the roast into a 10-inch pie plate tilting to coat the bottom and sides of pie plate. Pour in batter.

Bake 23 to 25 minutes or until the pudding is deep golden brown.

SERVE immediately with the roast.

YIELD: 8 servings

SOUR CREAM STREUSEL COFFEE CAKE

Unlike a ghost from the past, this delectable breakfast cake is no apparition. It was a familiar Sunday morning specialty at our house a decade ago, but its friendly presence needs to be rekindled for the throngs of young people who have not had the pleasure of enjoying Sour Cream Streusel Coffee Cake.

PREHEAT OVEN: 350 degrees F.

2 eggs, beaten	1 cup butter (margarine
1 teaspoon vanilla	may be used or use half
2 cups granulated sugar	of each)

Cream together the above ingredients, blending well.

ADD:

2 cups all purpose flour,
   1 teaspoon baking
   powder, 1 teaspoon salt

Mix thoroughly 2 to 3 minutes on medium speed of your electric mixer.

Recipe Continues...

SOUR CREAM STREUSEL COFFEE CAKE

Continued...

STREUSEL TOPPING:

2/3 cup chopped pecans
1 teaspoon ground
   cinnamon

1/4 teaspoon freshly ground
   nutmeg
1/2 cup brown sugar
5 tablespoons soft butter

Mix together with a fork until crumbly.

METHOD:

In bottom of greased and floured Bundt pan, place half of streusel mixture. Pour half of batter over. Top with remaining streusel mixture, then remainder of batter.

BAKE at 350 degrees F. 1 hour or until tested done. Cool before inverting onto serving plate.

BONUS: Can be made into two 5" x 9" loaves. Pour half of batter into greased and floured loaf pans. Top with one-half streusel mixture; remainder of batter, remaining streusel.

BAKE at 350 degrees F. for 40 to 45 minutes or until cakes test done.

Batter also makes great muffins.

P.S. If you haven't read my hints on greasing and flouring Bundt pans, etc. use "Baker's Joy" an oil and flour spray for baking pans. Can be found in "baking supply" aisle of most super markets.

OLYMPIC LIGHTS SCONES

If scones are a new experience for you, these are the ones to try. I have had many different makes and models and find these to be light, luscious and best of all, uncomplicated to produce.

4 cups all purpose flour
4 tablespoons granulated
   sugar
4 teaspoons baking powder
1 teaspoon baking soda
1 teaspoon salt
1 cup currents soaked in a
   little warm water or
   sherry (Drain and add to
   the flour.)

12 tablespoons cold butter

4 eggs
1 cup low fat buttermilk or
   1/2 buttermilk and 1/2 half
   and half

In a large bowl sift together the flour, sugar, baking powder, 1 teaspoon baking soda and 1 teaspoon salt.

Cut in the 12 tablespoons cold butter.

In a small bowl mix together the eggs and buttermilk.

Recipe Continued...

OLYMPIC LIGHTS SCONES
Continued...

Combine dry and wet ingredients and mix as little as possible to blend.
Divide the dough in half and place on a floured surface.
Pat into two 1/2-inch rounds.
Score each round into 12 pie-shaped wedges but don't cut all the way through the dough.

Place on ungreased cookie sheets. Brush with buttermilk and sprinkle generously with granulated sugar.

BAKE at 425 degrees F. about 12 minutes.

BONUS: We like the scones slightly warm. A special flavored coffee or spiced tea combine for a truly delectable flavor.

YIELD: 24 servings

LESLIE'S FAVORITE
POPPY SEED BREAD

Leslie likes to make this poppy seed bread to give as gifts, but her family usually devours a batch before she can sneak out of the house with any for herself or friends.

PREHEAT OVEN: 350 degrees F.

3 cups all purpose flour
2 cups granulated sugar
1-1/2 teaspoons baking
   powder
1-1/2 tablespoons poppy
   seed
1 teaspoon salt

1 cup plus 1 tablespoon
   Canola or other vegetable
   oil
3 eggs
1-1/2 teaspoons vanilla
1-1/2 teaspoons almond
   extract
1-1/2 cups milk

Mix together the dry ingredients in a large bowl. Whisk together the liquid ingredients and add to dry ingredients, mixing thoroughly. Spoon batter into two greased and floured loaf pans or 5 mini-loaf pans.

Bake at 350 degrees F. for 50 to 60 minutes.
Mini-loaves may take a little less time—check them carefully.

Recipe Continues...

LESLIE'S FAVORITE POPPY SEED BREAD

Continued...

Cool 5 minutes, then pour glaze over top. Let rest until all of the glaze has been absorbed.

GLAZE:

3/4 cup powdered sugar
2 tablespoons melted butter

1/4 cup orange juice
1/2 teaspoon almond extract

BONUS: Loaves freeze well. Flavor is enhanced by storing in refrigerator. Mini loaves are most popular and easy to slice.

YIELD: 2 regular loaves or 5 mini-loaves

DISTINCTIVELY PUMPKIN BREAD

This tastefully-put-together pumpkin bread is welcome at our house all year long. Let it become one of your favorites too!

PREHEAT OVEN: 350 degrees F.

1-1/2 cups granulated sugar
1/2 cup vegetable oil
1 cup canned pumpkin
1/4 cup water
2 eggs

1-2/3 cups all purpose flour

1/4 teaspoon baking powder
1 teaspoon baking soda
1/2 teaspoon salt
1/2 teaspoon cinnamon
1/2 teaspoon cloves
1/8 teaspoon fresh ground
   nutmeg

Mix together the first five ingredients. To this mixture add the remaining dry ingredients which have been sifted together.

Bake in a greased and floured egulation-size loaf pan at 350 degrees F. for 1 hour. Test for doneness as you would a cake.

Remove from oven to rack and cool before removing from pan.

BONUS: 1 cup chopped pecans creates a special treat. Also, the recipe doubles nicely and will net three slightly smaller normal-size loaves. Bread is amicable to freezer.

YIELD: 1 loaf (or 3 if recipe is doubled).

NONA JANE'S BATTER ROLLS

Everyone will enjoy making these delicious rolls because you don't "need to knead" the dough. Nona Jane goes through many dozens of these rolls at their cabin and says they are a Thanksgiving and Christmas tradition at the Van Dyck home.

1-1/2 cups warm water	4 cups all purpose flour
1/4 cup granulated sugar	1/3 cup soft shortening
2 packages dry yeast	1 egg
1-1/2 teaspoons baking soda	

Add yeast to warm water in bowl and let stand until dissolved. Add sugar, salt, shortening, egg and one-half of the flour. Beat for 2 minutes. Add rest of flour and mix. Cover and let rise for 30 to 60 minutes. Stir down batter.

Grease muffin tins and fill one-half full. Let rise until double (batter reaches top of tin).

Bake at 400 degrees for 10-15 minutes.

BONUS: Rising time depends on type of yeast and how fresh it is.

YIELD: About 30 rolls

PATTY'S ENGLISH CRUMPETS

The authentic English muffin. This recipe comes from my friend Patty who is still English by "trade." I call her the office alien. However, she has lived in the United States for over 25 years so that makes her solid American. English crumpets have more holes in them so one can use lots more butter to melt into all of the crevices. Once you try English Crumpets, you will have a hard time going back to our "bakery" made muffins.

1/2 ounce cake yeast (not powdered)
1 teaspoon salt
1 pint (English pint is 20 ounces) milk and water tepid

1 pound flour
Pinch of bicarbonate of soda (baking soda)

Cream yeast with small amount of tepid liquid. Slowly add remaining liquid, stirring constantly. Pour into flour, beating thoroughly with your hand, large wooden spoon, or large whisk for five minutes.

Cover and set in a warm place for one hour.

Dissolve baking soda and salt in a little warm water; add to the dough mixture. Beat again and let rise for another 45 minutes.

Recipe Continued...

222

PATTY'S ENGLISH CRUMPETS
Continued...

Grease griddle iron or very large heavy skillet and crumpet rings. Place rings on griddle/skillet and heat both until moderately hot. Pour enough batter into rings to cover bottoms completely. Cook until top is set (they will look dry and covered with air-holes). Remove rings; turn over on griddle and let bottoms dry a minute. Remove and turn back over. Let cool on rack, wrap and store.

To serve, pop them in the toaster to lightly brown the tops. Butter and serve with your favorite jams or marmalades. Yummy!

BONUS: The crumpet rings can be found in kitchen stores and some hardware stores. If you can't find rings—pour out batter as you would for pancakes.

—NOTES—

SOUPS, SALADS, ETC.:

SOUPS, SALADS, ETC.
Index

RED AND GREEN "HOLLY-DAY" SOUP

An ingenious, exciting soup to serve especially at Christmas. It is exciting to put together and your guests are sure to be amazed at your dexterity in performing such a fete.

RED SOUP:

1/4 cup butter
1 small onion, minced
1/4 cup all purpose flour
3 cups half-and half cream
3 cups crushed tomatoes—
   pureéd in food processor
   or blender

1/2 teaspoon crumbled dried
   basil
1/2 teaspoon garlic powder
   (optional)
Salt to taste

Melt butter in a 2-quart saucepan over medium heat and sauté the onion for 10 minutes. Sprinkle with flour. Gradually stir in half-and-half. Stir over medium heat until the mixture bubbles and thickens. Stir in the tomatoes, basil, garlic and salt to taste. Keep soup warm while making the Green Soup.

GREEN SOUP:

2 10-ounce packages
   frozen peas
6 cups chicken broth—home
   made or purchased

1/4 cup soft butter mixed
   with 1/4 cup all purpose
   flour
Salt, white pepper to taste
1 teaspoon dill weed
   (Tootie's suggestion)

Recipe Continues...

RED AND GREEN "HOLLY-DAY" SOUP
Continued...

GARNISH:

Fresh cilantro if available—
  minced

Combine peas and broth in a 2-quart saucepan. Simmer, covered, for 10 - 15 minutes. Remove from heat and pureé in blender or food processor. Return to saucepan, add the butter-flour mixture and stir over medium heat until soup thickens. Add seasoning.

Keep soup warm until ready to serve.

You will need two measuring cups for serving. Tootie says to fill measuring cups with enough soup to fill a soup bowl. Pour from each measuring cup at either side of a soup bowl simultaneously so the colors will remain separate. THIS IS THE FUN PART.

Garnish with the minced cilantro or parsley if cilantro is unavailable to you. I like to sprinkle the cilantro right down the center of the soup —from top to bottom or side to side. You are left to your imagination at this point.

Recipe Continues...

228

RED AND GREEN "HOLLY-DAY" SOUP
Continued...

BONUS: For a novel alternate garnish, using a small Christmas cookie cutter—such as a bell or tree—cut through a thin slice of white bread, toast and float on top of the soup.

P.S. Serve this beautiful soup for a holiday luncheon for your friends or use for children's Christmas party—making teddy bear cutouts or any other appropriate shape for the season. The cutouts could be a "project" for the "kids" at your house.

YIELD: 8 servings

TOMATO BISQUE

Perfect in color and taste—serve this very manageable holiday soup before your Christmas Eve dinner.

3 cups tomato juice
1 10-3/4 -ounce can
   condensed chicken broth
2 tablespoons brown sugar
1 teaspoon Worcestershire
   sauce

1/4 teaspoon celery salt
Dash of garlic—optional
1/8 teaspoon onion powder
1/4 cup dry sherry

In large saucepan mix together all of the ingredients except sherry. Bring to boiling.

Remove soup from heat and stir in sherry. Serve in individual soup bowls with oyster crackers.

BONUS: The sherry is optional but adds a bit of life to the tomato flavor. Doubling the soup works well.

YIELD: 6 to 8 servings

24 HOURS TO SALAD

A festive layered salad that you can prepare the day before or as I do, the night before your dinner party. This colorful salad will dazzle your guests and should be served on one of the 12 days before Christmas.

1 small head iceberg lettuce torn into bite-size pieces
1 small head Romaine or other leafy type lettuce torn into bite-size pieces
1/2 pound bacon crisply cooked and crumbled
1 small purple onion chopped
1 small bunch broccoli (florets only) chopped
1 10-ounce package frozen peas, thawed

1 medium size sweet red bell pepper, chopped
1 8-ounce can sliced water chestnuts, drained
1 small head cauliflower, chopped
1-1/2 cups shredded sharp cheddar cheese
1 cup low fat mayonnaise
1 cup low-fat sour cream

McCormick's Salad Supreme seasoning or other salad seasoning

GARNISH: Sweet red and green bell pepper rings

In a large clear glass salad bowl (trifle bowl works perfectly) start with the lettuce and layer in the order of ingredients given above. Be certain that the lettuce is not wet, otherwise salad will be limp.

Recipe Continues...

231

24 HOURS TO SALAD

Continued...

Mix the mayonnaise and sour cream together. After all of the salad ingredients are layered, sprinkle McCormick's Salad Supreme lightly over entire salad top. Then sprinkle 1 cup of the shredded cheddar cheese—then spread mayonnaise and sour cream to seal salad, seal to edge of bowl. Sprinkle Salad Supreme on top of this and then sprinkle on the last one-half cup of shredded cheddar cheese.

Cover the bowl tightly with plastic wrap, refrigerate up to 24 hours.

TOSS the salad at the table and garnish with the red and green pepper rings.

YIELD: Serves many—at least 16 servings

❧

MERRY, MERRY EGGNOG SALAD

Cranberries are traditionally holiday—so here's a salad that includes that festive berry.

1 envelope unflavored gelatin
1 8-ounce can crushed pineapple with juice
3 tablespoons lime juice
1-1/2 cups dairy eggnog
1/2 cup finely chopped celery

1-1/2 cups cranberry juice cocktail
1 3-ounce package raspberry-flavored gelatin
1 14-ounce jar cranberry-orange relish

In a medium saucepan combine the unflavored gelatin together with the undrained pineapple and the lime juice. Hold for 5 minutes; stir and cook over medium heat until gelatin is completely dissolved.

Remove from heat and cool mixture to room temperature. Stir in eggnog. Chill until partially set. Fold in the celery and turn into a 12" x 7" x 2" pan. Chill until barely firm.

Heat cranberry juice to boiling; stir in raspberry gelatine till dissolved. Chill until partially set. Fold in cranberry-orange relish. Spoon carefully on top of eggnog mixture. Chill until firm.

Cut into squares to serve. Arrange on lettuce leaves. Garnish with sugar-coated cranberries if desired.

BONUS: Substitute apple juice for the cranberry juice if desired.

YIELD: 12 servings

RASPBERRY VINAIGRETTE

Especially appropriate for the holidays, this raspberry flavored salad dressing can be enjoyed all year long.

1/4 cup granulated sugar
1/4 cup raspberry vinegar
   (homemade is best)
1 teaspoon dry mustard
1/4 teaspoon salt

3 green onions, finely
   chopped
1 tablespoon poppy seeds
1 cup Canola oil or oil of
   your choice

Combine the first six ingredients in a jar. Add the Canola oil. Cover the jar with a lid and shake until the sugar has dissolved. Store covered in refrigerator. Shake again before using.

BONUS: Dressing is more flavorful if held overnight or for at least 6 hours.

P.S. This vinaigrette is delicious served over a mixture of salad greens, toasted slivered almonds or pine nuts—if your budget can stand the strain—and cherry tomatoes.

P.P.S. "Best of Friends Vol. Too!" includes a recipe for raspberry vinegar.

YIELD: 8 generous servings

❧

RED AND GREEN VEGETABLE ASSORTMENT

This salad assortment is aptly named. Serve it at any one of the many holiday celebrations—perhaps it would be welcome on one of those marathon football-watching days.

MARINADE:

1-1/2 tablespoons fresh
  lemon juice
1-1/2 tablespoons raspberry
  or wine vinegar

4 tablespoons olive or
  canola oil

Put all of the dressing ingredients in a jar and shake well; pour dressing over veggies and marinate overnight.

VEGGIES:

2 cups thinly sliced
  cauliflower
1 cup broccoli florets
1/2 cup sliced stuffed green
  olives

1 green pepper—sliced in
  rings
1 sweet red bell pepper—
  sliced in rings

GALA CRANBERRY ICE

A beautiful holiday ice fancy enough to serve at a black tie event. Thanksgiving or Christmas are the perfect holidays to debut GALA CRANBERRY ICE.

About 3 hours before your dinner party, scoop out balls of this beautiful cranberry ice. Arrange in small crystal serving dishes and set back in the freezer. Cranberry ice may be served as a relish with turkey or even a prime rib roast, but don't forget that it will also make a dramatic entrance as dessert!

1 **pound bag fresh cranberries**	3-1/2 **cups water**
2 **cups granulated sugar**	1/2 **cup orange juice**
	1/4 **cup lemon juice.**

Place cranberries in a medium sauce pan with the sugar and water. Bring to boiling and simmer softly, stirring occasionally for 10 minutes. Cool, then press through a wire strainer and discard pulp. Add orange and lemon juice. Pour into a loaf pan, cover with foil and freeze.

BONUS: Obviously this festive ice can be made ahead of time for those unexpected "Guess who's coming to dinner" guests.

YIELD: 1 quart

CRANBERRY-ORANGE SALSA

Colorful and delicious, too, this cranberry specialty will be perfect for Thanksgiving or Christmas festivities. Especially tasteful with leftover turkey.

2 cups fresh cranberries
1 small seedless orange, peeled
2 jalapeño peppers, seeded and finely chopped
3 tablespoons minced crystallized (candied) ginger

3/4 cup granulated sugar
1/4 cup minced fresh mint (or dried if fresh unavailable)

This recipe is easiest to complete with a food processor, but a blender will suffice for the chopping.

Place slicing disc of your food processor in place; with processor running, press cranberries through food chute—using the food pusher and light pressure. Place sliced cranberries in a small bowl.

Replace the slicer with the knife blade and add the orange, peppers and ginger. Pulse 3 to 5 times or just until mixture is finely chopped. Be watchful so mixture does not get real mushy.

Recipe Continues...

CRANBERRY-ORANGE SALSA

Continued...

Add to cranberries, stir in sugar and mint.

Store in glass containers in refrigerator.

BONUS: Crystallized ginger can be found in the Chinese food section of most super markets or where oriental products are sold. Ask your grocer to order it for you if it is "totally" unavailable in your area.

YIELD: 2 cups

SWEET POTATOES STUFFED

These disparate potatoes are delicious any time of the year.
They are excellent soul mates to old-fashioned baked ham.

6 medium sweet potatoes or
yams (6 ounces each)
2 tablespoons butter
1/4 cup orange marmalade
1/4 teaspoon salt
1/2 teaspoon ground
cinnamon

1/4 teaspoon freshly ground
nutmeg
1/3 cup finely chopped
walnuts (optional)

Scrub the potatoes; prick with a fork. Bake in a 425 degree F. oven for 40 to 60 minutes or just till tender.

Cut a lengthwise slice from the tops of each potato. Remove skin from the slices and place the pulp into a medium mixing bowl.

Scoop out each potato leaving a 1/4-inch shell. Add pulp to the mixing bowl.

Mash potatoes adding butter or margarine, marmalade, salt, and spices. With electric mixer, mash the potatoes. Spoon mixture back into potato shells. Sprinkle the chopped nuts on top if desired.

Recipe Continues...

239

SWEET POTATOES STUFFED

Continued...

BONUS: These yummy potatoes can be made ahead, covered and refrigerated up to 24 hours. Bake covered in a 425 degree F. oven for 30 to 40 minutes or until heated through.

To serve at once, place in a baking dish. Bake uncovered in a 425 degree F. oven for 10 to 15 minutes.

To microwave, arrange in a circle on microwave-safe 12-inch pizza plate. Microcook uncovered on 100% power for 6 to 8 minutes.

YIELD: 6 servings

ELEGANT FRUITED SLAW

You can plan ahead by preparing your side dishes 24 hours in advance of serving. I think this fruit slaw is an excellent choice for that extraordinary holiday buffet. Watch it disappear in the blink of Santa's big brown eyes.

A straight-sided glass bowl will show this salad off in grand style.

3 cups finely shredded
  cabbage—red would
  be nice
2 cups finely shredded
  iceberg lettuce
1 teaspoon poppy seeds
1 15-1/4-ounce can
  pineapple tidbits, drained
1-1/2 cups seedless red
  grapes—halved
1 medium cantaloupe,
  peeled, seeded and cut
  into balls or cubes

(If cantaloupe is
unavailable in your area
at Christmas, frozen
melon balls are usually
available in the frozen-
food section of your local
super market.)
1 8-oz. carton lemon
  flavored yogurt
1/4 cup low fat mayonnaise
  or salad dressing
Freshly grated nutmeg
Shredded orange peel
Pecan halves

Toss the cabbage, lettuce and poppy seeds together.
In a straight-sided 3-quart clear glass bowl or soufflé dish, place 1/3 of the cabbage mixture. Top with a layer of pineapple. Add grapes evenly over the pineapple. Top with a second layer of the cabbage mixture. Layer melon balls over second layer and top with remaining cabbage mixture.

Recipe Continues...

ELEGANT FRUITED SLAW

Continued...

Stir together the lemon yogurt, mayonnaise or salad dressing and ground nutmeg. Spread over top layer, covering all of the cabbage to the edges of the bowl.

Cover with plastic wrap and chill up to 24 hours.

Just before serving, sprinkle with shredded orange peel and top with the pecan halves. Toss the salad carefully just before serving.

BONUS: Don't forget to take a picture of your sumptuous buffet table.

YIELD: 12 servings

PIQUANT WILD RICE DRESSING

If you are considering changing your traditional holiday dressing, try using wild rice. It has a nutty flavor and crunchy texture that is unsurpassable. It is easy to prepare and keeps for months when frozen.

1 cup wild rice
3 cups chicken broth or
   3 bouillon cubes in
   3 cups boiling water
1 cup diced celery
1/4 cup minced onion
1/2 cup butter or margarine
   melted

1 4-ounce can mushrooms
   or 1/3 cup fresh sliced
   mushrooms
1/4 teaspoon salt
1/4 teaspoon pepper
1/4 teaspoon sage
1/4 teaspoon thyme

Cook wild rice by boiling in 3 cups chicken broth for 40 minutes stovetop. Do not overcook. Sauté the celery, onion and fresh mushrooms in butter for 2-3 minutes. Combine all ingredients including the cooked wild rice.

This recipe makes about 6 cups of dressing and is enough to stuff a 10-pound turkey.

BONUS: I prepare the dressing and spoon it into a buttered baking dish. Bake covered at 350 degrees F. for 1 hour.

If desired, one pound fresh country sausage may be browned, drained and added to the dressing for a "wild" variety.

YIELD: 6 cups without sausage

CORN BREAD DRESSING, COUNTRY STYLE

Here's the dressing to try out posthaste. My family enjoys as a side dish rather than "stuffed into a bird." It is especially yummy served with chicken gravy, country style.

1 cup chopped white onion
1 cup chopped celery with some of the leaves
1/4 cup water
6 cups crumbled corn bread
6 slices toasted "regular" bread, torn into small pieces

5 eggs—beaten slightly
1 tablespoon ground sage
1 cup cubed cooked turkey or chicken
1/4 teaspoon seasoned salt
2 to 2-1/2 cups chicken broth, purchased or home made

Cook the onion and celery in water for about 5 minutes; drain. Combine the corn bread, regular bread, cooked onion and celery, eggs, sage, salt and cooked chicken or turkey. Stir in enough of the chicken broth to make the stuffing extra moist. Turn into a greased 8" x 8" x 2" baking dish.

Bake, covered, at 400 degrees F. for 30 minutes. Uncover and bake another 5 to 10 minutes more until dressing is heated through and the top is a little crusty.

Recipe Continues...

CORN BREAD DRESSING, COUNTRY STYLE

Continued...

BONUS: If you don't have any leftover chicken or turkey in your refrigerator, stop by the local deli and pick up just enough to add to this extra-special corn bread delight.

Also, this dressing can be made early in the day. Cover and refrigerate until ready to bake.

YIELD: Depending on how ravenous your dinner pals are—6 to 8 servings

ARTICHOKE HEARTS AND SHRIMP

My very favorite combination. This easy and elegant appeteaser or buffet side dish can definitely be accomplished the night before your gala event be it New Year's Day or Christmas Eve. It is a very substantial side dish to accompany cold turkey, sliced ham or any other entree that needs company. I personally can make a meal of artichokes and shrimp by simply adding a special mini-biscuit or muffin.

1/2 cup vegetable oil
1/4 cup white wine vinegar
3 tablespoons dry white wine
2 teaspoons parsley—fresh or dried
1/2 teaspoon granulated sugar
1/4 teaspoon salt
1/4 teaspoon paprika
1/8 teaspoon whole black peppercorns
1/2 clove garlic, minced (optional)

1 pound medium shrimp, cooked, peeled and deveined
1 9-ounce package frozen artichokes, thawed and halved/or one
14-ounce can artichoke hearts in water, drained and halved
1/2 small onion, peeled and sliced into rings
1/2 cup sliced water chestnuts, drained

In a large jar with lid, combine salad oil, vinegar, wine, parsley, sugar, salt, paprika, peppercorns and garlic; cover and shake to blend well.

Recipe Continues...

ARTICHOKE HEARTS AND SHRIMP
Continued...

In a large glass bowl combine the shrimp, artichoke hearts, onion and water chestnuts; pour marinade over this mixture. Cover and refrigerate overnight or at least 12 hours.

BONUS: Depending upon the season, frozen artichoke hearts are hard to come by. The canned ones run a close second to being perfect so don't hesitate to use them.

YIELD: 8 - 10 servings

TURKEY FRAME SOUP & NOODLES

Actually, this "leftover" turkey frame soup should be called "framed turkey" because the turkey didn't know it was going to be raised for making soup. If you have a nice "meaty" turkey frame left over at Thanksgiving or Christmas, try this excellent example.

5 quarts water
1 meaty turkey frame
1 medium onion, quartered
4 teaspoons salt
Pepper to taste

3 medium tomatoes,
    quartered
1 teaspoon dried thyme,
    crushed
1/2 teaspoon dried oregano,
    crushed

1/2 teaspoon fennel
    (optional)

8 cups fresh vegetables,
    chopped or sliced
    (any combination of
    chopped celery, carrots,
    onion, broccoli, shredded
    cabbage, or cauliflower)

Old fashioned home made noodles (recipe follows)

In a large Dutch oven or soup kettle place the "framed turkey" with the quartered onion, 5 quarts of water, salt and pepper. Bring to boiling. Reduce heat; cover and simmer for 1-1/2 hours. Remove the frame and cool until easy to handle. Remove meat from bones; discard the "bare bones."

Recipe Continues...

248

TURKEY FRAME SOUP & NOODLES

Continued...

Strain broth. Return meat to broth with tomatoes, and seasonings. Stir in the desired vegetables. Bring to boiling, cover and simmer for 45 minutes. Return to boiling and add the noodles. Boil uncovered for about 15 minutes or until noodles are tender.

OLD FASHIONED NOODLES: In a large bowl combine 1 beaten egg, 2 tablespoons milk and 1/2 teaspoon salt. Add enough all purpose flour (1 to 1-1/4 cups) to make a fairly stiff dough. On a lightly floured surface, roll out the dough until thin. Let stand for 20 minutes. Roll up loosely. Slice noodles 1/4 inch wide. Unroll cut noodles; spread out to dry—about two hours.

BONUS: If you are not in the mood to make the noodles, it is certainly okay to use "grocery store" noodles. Chances are, you have a pasta-making machine in your kitchen which is also permissible. Enjoy!!

YIELD: 12 generous servings

–NOTES–

ENTREÉS:

ENTREÉS
Index

BOBBIE'S CHRISTMAS EVE ROAST BEEF

No one will "beef" about this exceptionally festive Christmas Eve dinner. Plan early by coercing your favorite butcher to save you an especially marvelous cut of prime rib—either with "bone" or boneless, rolled and tied. I prefer to buy a standing rib roast—it is definitely more impressive.

DON'T BE SCARED AWAY BY THE FOLLOWING INSTRUCTIONS. Trust me. I will lead you down the path from buying the roast to serving it.

One 8 to 9-pound standing rib roast (should serve 8 to 10)

PREHEAT OVEN: 325 degrees F.

You will need a shallow roasting pan with a rack if available. You will not need a lid—it will be "open pan roasted."

Mix the following seasonings together for rubbing on the roast.

1/2 **teaspoon salt**	1/4 **teaspoon dried basil**
1/4 **teaspoon dried marjoram leaves**	**leaves**
	1/4 **teaspoon rubbed savory**
1/4 **teaspoon dried thyme leaves**	**(optional)**
	1/4 **teaspoon black pepper**

Recipe Continues...

253

BOBBIE'S CHRISTMAS EVE ROAST BEEF
Continued...

The listed seasonings are not difficult to come by. Most grocers stock them.

—————————

1 teaspoon liquid gravy seasoning (such as Kitchen Bouquet)
1/2 cup red burgundy wine (a dry red wine—not very expensive)

Stand the roast in roasting pan. Rub salt mixture into the beef on all sides. If you have a meat thermometer, insert it through the outside fat into the thickest part of muscle—the point should not rest on fat or bone.

Mix the gravy seasoning with Burgundy and spoon some of it over the beef.

Roast uncovered, basting several times with the remaining Burgundy mixture. If you don't have a baster, just use a large spoon to baste the roast and ask Santa Claus for a baster next year.

Cook until desired doneness.

Rare equals 140 degrees F. or 3-1/2 hours
Medium is 160 degrees F. or 4-1/2 hours
Well-done is 170 degrees F. or 5 hours

Remove cooked roast to heated platter. Pour drippings into a 2-cup measuring cup. Hold aside the roast while making the gravy. It will slice easier if it sets at least 20 minutes.

Recipe Continues...

BOBBIE'S CHRISTMAS EVE ROAST BEEF
Continued...

BURGUNDY GRAVY:

6 tablespoons roast
  drippings
1/4 cup unsifted all purpose
  flour
1/2 teaspoon salt
sprinkling of pepper

2 10-1/2-ounce cans of
  condensed beef bouillon
  (in soup section of your
  grocery store)
1/2 cup burgundy wine

RETURN the 6 tablespoons reserved roast-beef drippings to the roasting pan. Stir in the flour, salt and pepper to make a smooth mixture. Slowly add the beef bouillon and burgundy to the flour mixture, stirring until it gets smooth and browned bits from the roast are dissolved.

Bring to boiling, stirring. Reduce heat and continue stirring for 5 minutes. Taste to determine if it needs more salt.

Serve in separate bowl (or gravy boat if you have one).

You should end up with about 3 cups of burgundy gravy.

Recipe Continues...

BOBBIE'S CHRISTMAS EVE ROAST BEEF

Continued...

BONUS: Yorkshire pudding (more like a bread) is traditionally served with prime rib roast. I personally don't care for it. Popovers are favored by my family. The recipes for both are in this book so you can choose for yourself. You may choose either or neither—do your own thing.

P.S. You can order any size roast you need. Usually rule-of-thumb for standing rib roast is one pound per person because of the weight of the bone vs. the meat.

YIELD: 8 - 10 servings

DELSEA'S CHICKEN CURRY

Delsea just made it by the "tip of her chinny, chin, chin!" However, her chicken curry recipe is definitely a "keeper," and should be accomplished for any occasion—festive or otherwise. How about your turn for Gourmet Club? This is an exciting and festive dish to concoct. Don't let the length of ingredients deter you. They are readily available at most super markets.

Two 3-1/2 pound baking
  chickens
Salt, fresh ground pepper,
  lemon juice
2 ounces butter
1/4 cup extra-virgin olive oil
2 yellow onions, sliced
1 large carrot, chopped
2 pieces celery
1 green apple, cored,
  sliced, skin on
4 tablespoons Indian curry
  powder
4 tablespoons all purpose
  flour
1 teaspoon tomato paste
1 teaspoon Bovril® meat
  glaze or Kitchen Bouquet®

2-1/2 cups chicken stock—
  home made or purchased
1 teaspoon lemon juice
1 teaspoon shredded
  coconut
1 tablespoon honey
2 tablespoons guava jelly
  (or pineapple)
1 small cinnamon stick
1 small piece fresh ginger
  root
3 crushed cardamom seeds
1 large clove garlic
1 whole clove
1/2 teaspoon dry mustard
Salt and cayenne to taste

Recipe Continues...

DELSEA'S CHICKEN CURRY
Continued...

Bake chickens after seasoning inside with salt, lemon juice and freshly ground pepper. Let cool and bone. (No skin or bones, just nice bite size pieces.) Cover and set aside in container to seal later.

Heat olive oil and vegetable oil in heavy skillet with butter. Add sliced onions, carrot, celery and apple. Stir, cover and cook 5 minutes. Add curry, stir and cook for another 5 minutes. Stir in flour and cook 5 minutes.

Remove from heat, add tomato paste, meat glaze, chicken stock, lemon juice, coconut, honey, guava jelly, cinnamon stick, ginger root, cardamom, garlic clove, dry mustard, salt and cayenne. Stir until it comes to a boil and simmer for at least one hour.

"Rub" through strainer and pour the "juicy" paste over boned pieces of chicken. Cover and refrigerate. Heat up when ready to use.

Serve with rice and have lots of condiments, such as chutney, chopped fresh pineapple, chopped onion, chopped egg, currants, coconut, chopped peanuts, chopped dates, chopped apple, etc. Use your imagination.

BONUS: Delsea says that this dish is best prepared the day before serving and even better when 1 to 2 days old!!!

This recipe was the last one to be written for Volume 3, "Best of Friends Festive Occasions." It just made the deadline for press time and is written as given to me by Delsea. ENJOY!!!

YIELD: 8 servings

❦

SHERRIED CHICKEN

This oven-baked chicken is definitely for the "harried." It is a quick and easy recipe and elegantly presentable. Your family will definitely want it served frequently—your guests will ask for the recipe.

2 2-1/2 pound broiler-
   fryers—cut in pieces
   (skinned)
   or as I prefer—skinless,
   boneless chicken breasts
1 medium onion chopped
   and sautéed in vegetable
   oil
1/4 pound fresh mushrooms,
   sliced and sautéed in
   vegetable oil

1 10-1/2-ounce can cream of
   mushroom soup
1 cup (1/2 pint) low fat sour
   cream
1/4 cup dry cooking sherry
Salt and freshly ground
   pepper to taste

PREHEAT OVEN: 350 degrees F.

Arrange the chicken in a single layer in large shallow casserole dish or a roasting pan. Combine remainder of ingredients which have been mixed together and pour over top of the chicken.
Bake 45 minutes to an hour. Baste as necessary throughout the baking time.

Recipe Continues...

SHERRIED CHICKEN
Continued...

BONUS: You can choose whatever "parts" of chicken are best suited to the occasion - your family may enjoy legs. I prefer to serve skinless chicken breasts whenever I do chicken dishes.

Also, many of the cream soups are now available in no sodium, low fat versions—they are perfect for making sauces.

P.S. If your family doesn't like cream of mushroom soup, you can substitute cream of chicken or cream of celery soup.

YIELD: 6 to 8 servings—depending on how many pieces of chicken you use

❧

DISTINGUISHED TENDERLOIN

Delicious and impressive. This tenderloin needs no special tactics to prepare. Even the novice cook can accomplish this wonderful entreé without undue effort.

PREHEAT OVEN: 400 degrees F.

Have your butcher cut a 4 pound whole beef tenderloin.

2 to 3 tablespoons softened butter	2 tablespoons low sodium soy sauce
	1 teaspoon Dijon mustard
1/4 cup chopped scallions or green onions	Pepper to taste
2 tablespoons butter	3/4 cup dry sherry

Spread the tenderloin with softened butter and using a shallow roasting pan (or broiler pan) bake uncovered for to 20 to 30 minutes.

While the tenderloin is cooking as above, sauté the scallions or green onions in the remaining 2 tablespoons butter. Add the soy sauce, mustard and pepper. Add the sherry, stirring until just boiling.

After the tenderloin has cooked 20 or 30 minutes, pour the above sauce over all and bake another 30 minutes to serve medium rare. Bake longer if you want the roast cooked to medium well; baste roast often.

Recipe Continues...

DISTINGUISHED TENDERLOIN
Continued...

After removing roast from oven, let it rest for 10 minutes. Carve in 1-inch slices and arrange on warmed platter with a scattering of mushrooms for a luxuriant garnish. Serve your favorite wine sauce or a nice bernaise in separate gravy boats.

BONUS: You will find an extremely delicious bernaise sauce in Volume 1 "Best of Friends, Etc." Also, there are many such packaged sauces available at your super market. Also featured in this cookbook is a "Friendly Wine Sauce" befitting your most celebrated guests.

YIELD: 8 -10 servings

FRIENDLY WINE SAUCE

A faultless wine sauce to serve with your favorite beef entreé!

6 tablespoons butter
1/2 pound fresh mushrooms, sliced
2 small onions, finely chopped
1 clove garlic (optional) minced
3 tablespoons bottled chili sauce
1/2 teaspoon all purpose flour

A scattering of dried marjoram and thyme
3 drops Tabasco
3 splashes of Worcestershire sauce
4 to 5 ounces dry red wine such as burgundy
1 tablespoon bouillon dissolved in 1/4 cup warm water
Salt and pepper to taste

Melt butter in large skillet. Add mushrooms, onions and garlic if used. Sauté until onions are just soft. Add all remaining ingredients and mix well. Just simmer for 10 minutes.

Serve hot in sauce boat.

❧

PORK MEDALLIONS IN MUSHROOM-BEER SAUCE

These saucy pork medallions provide an alternative to the hum-drum days of beef or chicken and are particularly appropriate for that special dinner party for someone special.

1 stick butter
Flour for coating pork
  medallions

8 pork medallions, 1/2-inch
  thick

1 cup chopped green onions
1 cup sliced fresh
  mushrooms

1/2 teaspoon dried thyme
1 12-ounce can beer
Salt
Freshly ground pepper

Buttered noodles
Minced fresh parsley for
  garnish

Heat butter in a large skillet until foamy; flour medallions and brown well on both sides. Remove and set aside. Add onion and garlic to skillet; sauté 2 minutes. Add mushrooms and thyme; sauté an additional 3 minutes. Return medallions to skillet and add beer; bring to a boil. Reduce heat, cover and simmer for 1 hour. Season with salt and pepper. Arrange chops on platter of hot buttered noodles. Cover with sauce and garnish with the chopped parsley.

BONUS: Have your butcher cut boneless pork tenderloin slices for the pork medallions.

YIELD: 8 servings

PEPPERED BEEFSTEAKS WITH JACK DANIELS SAUCE

Another one of Marilyn's intimate dinner for two specials. What an exciting surprise for that specific sweetheart. Keep it in mind for Valentine's Day or for a "just because" dinner at home.

2 tablespoons minced shallot	2 8-ounce beef tenderloin steaks
1 tablespoon red wine vinegar	1/2 teaspoon dried thyme, crumbled
3-1/2 teaspoons cracked black pepper	1/2 teaspoon dried marjoram, crumbled
2 cups beef stock or canned unsalted broth	1/4 cup extra virgin olive oil
1 cup chicken stock or canned low-salt broth	1 tablespoon Jack Daniels whiskey or other whiskey

Boil shallot, vinegar and 1-1/2 teaspoons pepper in heavy medium sauce pan until almost no liquid remains in pan; about 1 minute. Add both stocks and boil until reduced to 1/2 cup, about 20 minutes. (Sauce can be prepared 1 day ahead. Cover and refrigerate.)

Place steaks in baking dish. Rub remaining 2 teaspoons pepper and herbs onto both sides of steaks. Pour oil over steaks, turn to coat. Cover and let stand 1 hour at room temperature.

Recipe Continues...

PEPPERED BEEFSTEAKS WITH JACK DANIELS SAUCE

Continued...

Remove meat from marinade. Heat heavy large skillet on medium high and cook to desired doneness, about 3 minutes per side for rare. Transfer steaks to plates. Add sauce to skillet and bring to boil. Mix in Jack Daniels, spoon over steaks and serve.

BONUS: Serve with a crispy tossed salad and perhaps a twice-baked potato. And—don't forget something chocolate for dessert. Perhaps a slice of decadent Turtle Cheesecake from Volume "Too!" would be just decadent enough.

YIELD: For two only!

❧

CHICKEN AND VEGETABLES

A recipe that receives rave reviews whenever served. Easily prepared—it only needs a fruit salad and muffins to complete the menu. Be prepared to receive compliments on your cooking abilities.

4 whole chicken breasts
4 cups chicken stock
  (water, 3 stalks celery—

chopped, 1/2 small onion
chopped)

Cover and poach chicken in stock until tender which should be about 30 minutes. Cool and reserve stock. Remove skin from chicken and bone. Cut chicken in bite-size cubes and set aside.

TOPPING:

1/2 cup butter
1 cup diced celery
1 cup diced onion
1/2 cup reserved chicken
  stock
1 tablespoon leaf sage,
  crushed

4-1/2 cups Pepperidge Farm
  Herb-Seasoned Stuffing
  (or other similar brand)
Salt and freshly ground
  pepper to taste

Melt butter in a large skillet, add celery and onion and sauté until transparent. Blend in chicken stock, sage and prepared stuffing. Add salt and pepper to taste. Set aside.

Recipe Continues...

CHICKEN AND VEGETABLES
Continued...

VEGETABLES:

1-1/2 cups sliced fresh
  mushrooms
1/2 cup minced fresh parsley

1 10-ounce package frozen
  tiny peas, defrosted

Toss together in bowl (peas do not need to be cooked).

SAUCE:

2 10-1/2-ounce cans cream
  of chicken soup
1 cup low fat dairy sour
  cream

1/3 cup chicken stock

Blend all ingredients together; set aside.

In a 9" x 13" shallow baking dish, layer 2/3 of the topping; cover with chicken and vegetables. Pour sauce over all. Sprinkle remaining stuffing mixture on top. Cover and bake for 30 minutes or until hot and bubbly.

BONUS: To "poach" chicken breasts means to cover chicken with the water etc., cover, and simmer over medium heat for 30 minutes. (Check with fork for doneness).

YIELD: 8 servings

TURKEY AND SWISS

Sounds like something one would order from the corner Deli; however, this innovative cheesecake is actually okay for brunch or lunch. Who said cheesecake was for dessert only??

1/4 cup buttery cracker crumbs
9 ounces (2-1/4 cups) shredded Swiss cheese (hold 1/4 cup aside)
1/4 cup margarine, melted
2 8-ounce packages low fat cream cheese, softened
4 large eggs

1/4 cup all purpose flour
1 carton (8 ounces) dairy sour cream (low fat)
1/2 teaspoon ground sage
1/4 teaspoon ground white pepper
3 cups finely diced cooked turkey—leftovers or deli cooked

Brandied cranberry sauce (recipe found elsewhere in this volume)

Blend together the breadcrumbs, 1/4 cup Swiss cheese and butter; stir well. Firmly press mixture on bottom of a 9-inch springform pan. Set aside.

Beat the cream cheese at high speed in electric mixer bowl until creamy. Add eggs one at a time, beating very well after each addition. Add flour and sour cream, sage and white pepper. Beat on low speed until smooth. Stir in remaining 2 cups Swiss cheese and the turkey. Pour batter into prepared pan.

Recipe Continues...

TURKEY AND SWISS

Continued...

BAKE at 350 degrees F. for 55 to 60 minutes or until center of cheesecake is is set and not "wiggly."

Remove from oven, cool 30 minutes on wire rack.

Carefully remove sides of springform pan snd serve in wedges with warmed brandied cranberry sauce to the side.

BONUS: A nice crusty bread is a nice tag-along if the cheesecake is served as an entree.

❦

TURKEY GRAVY

This Southern style creamy turkey gravy is not the "norm." I like it for a change and if you have good pan drippings, this gravy is the one to dazzle your holiday guests.

Hot drippings from roast turkey
1/4 cup all purpose flour
1-1/4 teaspoons dried sage, crushed

1/8 teaspoon ground red pepper
Salt to taste
Milk or light cream

Transfer roast turkey to a serving platter; keep warm. Leave any crusty bits in the roasting pan, pour pan drippings into a large measuring cup. Skim off fat from drippings.

Return 1/4 cup of the fat to the roasting pan; discard any remaining. Stir in the flour, sage, salt and red pepper. Cook and stir over medium low heat just until bubbly. Remove from heat and add enough milk to the drippings in the liquid measuring cup to equal 2-3/4 cups total. Add all to the flour mixture in pan. Return to heat and cook until thickened and bubbly—stirring constantly.

BONUS: You can adjust the measurements to double the recipe. You should have enough drippings to do so. Also, if you prefer, use black pepper instead of the red pepper above.

YIELD: 2-1/2 cups

–NOTES–

DESSERTS:

DESSERTS
Index

CROWNING GLORY

Pam's favorite recipe to end a spectacular festive occasion, this chocolate-filled cream puff ring is luscious, light and best of all, easy to complete. Once you prepare this cream puff, you will most likely put this recipe at the top of your list for other special occasions.

Chocolate-filled Cream-Puff Ring

1 recipe cream-puff paste   Chocolate Glaze
Chocolate Filling   Sliced Almonds
     Whipped Cream

Butter a 9-inch circle on cookie sheet. Drop paste by 1/4 measuring-cupfuls just inside circumference of circle so that it forms a ring, or force paste through a pastry bag fitted with wide-mouthed tube, forming 2 rings, one inside the other, to make the base; continue piping remaining puff paste in layers until completely used.

Bake in preheated 400 degree F. oven for 40 minutes or until puffed and well browned. Cool on rack.

A few hours before serving, carefully slice the ring crosswise with long, sharp, thin-bladed knife. Gently lift off top. Fill with chocolate filling and replace top. Drizzle with chocolate glaze, then sprinkle top with almonds.

Recipe Continues...

CROWNING GLORY
Continued...

Chill several hours or until ready to serve. Serve with small dollop of whipped cream.

YIELD: 12 servings

Cream-puff Paste

1 cup water
1/2 cup butter or margarine
1 teaspoon sugar

1/4 teaspoon salt
1 cup all purpose flour
14 large eggs

Combine water, butter, sugar and salt in heavy saucepan and bring to boil. Add flour all at once and then beat with wooden spoon over low heat 1 minute or until mixture leaves sides of pan and forms a mixture that does not separate.

Remove from heat and beat about 2 minutes to cool mixture slightly. Add eggs one at a time, beating after each until mixture has satin-like sheen.

Chocolate Filling

1 cup butter or margarine,
  softened
1 cup granulated sugar
4 ounces unsweetened
  chocolate squares, melted
  and cooled

2 teaspoons vanilla extract
6 eggs

Recipe Continues...

276

CROWNING GLORY
Continued...

In a mixer bowl, cream butter and sugar until light and fluffy. Beat in chocolate and vanilla, then add eggs one at a time, beating 2 minutes after each. Continue to beat until sugar is thoroughly dissolved, then chill.

Chocolate Glaze

In top of double boiler over hot, not boiling, water melt 2 squares semi-sweet chocolate and 2 tablespoons butter or margarine, stirring to combine.

Whipped Cream

Beat 1 cup heavy cream and 2 tablespoons sugar until stiff. Serve with ring. For chocolate-flavored whipped cream, add powdered unsweetened cocoa to taste while beating.

THREE FEATHERS INN— STICKY TOFFEE PUDDING

Adapted for American measurements—a perfect holiday dessert.

CAKE:

6 oz. pitted dates, chopped	6 oz granulated sugar
1 level teaspoon baking soda	4 tablespoons butter
1 cup water	6 oz self-rising flour
2 eggs	1/2 teaspoon vanilla extract

Pour water over dates, bring to a boil, add baking soda and set aside. Cream butter and sugar, adding eggs, flour, dates and liquid plus vanilla extract.

Grease an 8-inch square cake pan

Bake at 350 degrees F. for 35 - 40 minutes.

SAUCE:

1 cup packed brown sugar	4-1/2 ounces butter
1 cup whipping cream	1/2 teaspoon vanilla extract

Recipe Continues...

THREE FEATHERS INN— STICKY TOFFEE PUDDING

Continued...

Place all ingredients in saucepan and simmer for 3 minutes. Pour a little over the warm cake and return to oven to bubble. Cut cake into small squares and pass the warm sauce separately.

BONUS: Cake freezes nicely as well as the butterscotch sauce.

YIELD: 12 servings

ANGEL CHERRY PIE

This is an especially appropriate dessert for the holiday season. It, however, is delectable any time of the year.

2 eggs, separated
1/4 teaspoon cream of tartar
1 cup granulated sugar
1 envelope unflavored
 gelatin
1/4 cup water
1 pint (2 cups) small curd
 cottage cheese

1/2 teaspoon grated lemon
 peel
2 tablespoons lemon juice
1 can (21 oz.) cherry pie
 filling

In a small mixer bowl, beat the egg whites and cream of tartar until frothy; beat in 1/2 cup of the sugar—1 tablespoon at a time—and continue beating until stiff and glossy. Be careful not to overbeat.

Evenly spread the meringue in a well-buttered 9-inch pie plate, pushing up against the sides.

BAKE at 275 degrees F. for 45 minutes, remove from oven and cool.

Recipe Continues...

ANGEL CHERRY PIE

Continued

Meanwhile in a medium saucepan, soften the gelatin in water for 5 minutes; add the remaining 1/2 cup sugar and stir over medium heat until the gelatin and sugar are completely dissolved. In a blender whirl the cottage cheese, lemon peel and juice. Add the egg yolks and beat until smooth. Add the gelatin mixture and whirl to combine. Chill until mixture mounds a bit on top of a spoon. Pour this mixture into the cooled meringue shell; chill until set. Spoon the pie filling over top of the pie and chill again until serving.

BONUS: If you bake the meringue pie shell ahead, fill it early on the day you plan to serve it.

YIELD: 6 - 8 servings

❦

CRANBERRY/PEAR CRISP

Particularly perfect for the holidays when cranberries are fresh and winter pears are scrumptious. Its unique flavors will capture you and those who partake.

FILLING:

3-1/2 pounds ripe pears
   (about 7 pears)
   each peeled, cored, cut
   lengthwise into eight
   slices
1 cup fresh cranberries
1/2 cup granulated sugar

2 tablespoons unbleached
   all purpose flour
1/2 teaspoon ground
   cinnamon
1/4 teaspoon freshly ground
   nutmeg

TOPPING:

1 cup all purpose flour
2/3 cup firmly packed
   golden brown sugar
1/2 cup old fashioned rolled
   oats

1/4 teaspoon salt
1 stick sweet butter
   (1/2 cup) cut into pieces

PREHEAT OVEN to 350 degrees F.

Butter an 8-inch square baking dish.

Recipe Continues...

282

CRANBERRY/PEAR CRISP
Continued...

FOR TOPPING:

Combine all ingredients except butter. Add butter and cut in using fork, fingertips or a pastry blender. Mixture should resemble pebbles.

FOR FILLING:

Toss all filling ingredients together in a bowl to combine well. Transfer filling to baking dish, scatter topping mix evenly atop filling.

Set dish on baking sheet and transfer to center of oven rack and bake until topping is lightly browned and bubbling juices are thickened. Dessert should bake approximatcly 1 hour.

Cool and serve with whipped cream or vanilla ice cream.

BONUS: Frozen cranberries may be used.

YIELD: 6 generous servings

LEMON SILK

*If you like lemon, this is just what the doctor ordered.
Besides being simply delicious, it is simple in its creation.*

PREHEAT OVEN: 325 degrees F.

3 eggs
1 cup granulated sugar
2 tablespoons flour
2 lemons—1/3 cup juice

Finely grated peel of 1
  lemon
1 cup 2% milk

Butter 6 custard cups. Beat the eggs, sugar and flour until mixture is very thick. Blend in the lemon juice and peel, then add milk. Pour into cups. Fill cups close to top of rim. Set in cake pan or other baking dish and add hot water halfway up the sides of cups.

Bake until top is firm—about 45 minutes. Chill completely before serving.

BONUS: Garnish with a bit of whipped cream and a "sprinkle of LEMON ZEST!! This is a good time to explain lemon "zest." When a recipe calls for zest—whether it be lime, lemon, grapefruit or orange—it means the colored part of the fruit without the "pith" or white underpart of the peeling. You can purchase a "zesting" tool at most kitchen stores or perhaps a hardware store where they carry cooking utensils, etc. It has three or four little holes at the bottom

Recipe Continues...

LEMON SILK

Continued...

of its handle—you pull this across the lemon or whatever fruit you are using—and you will get the finest little strips of "zest." Some people also enjoy a bit of "zest" with certain cocktails or with plain seltzer, etc. If you don't have a "zester" tool—you can accomplish the same with a vegetable peeler by cutting strips from the fruit.

This recipe calls for finely grated lemon peel. I grate the peel of one lemon and then chop it fine in my food processor. It is easiest to perform your grating, zesting or peeling before juicing the lemon, etc. Also, you will get more juices from lemons, etc. if they are at room temperature.

P.S. I couldn't wait to taste the Lemon Silk—so I ate mine while it was still warm— "to die for." I also think a meringue topping would be absolutely wonderful! Add the meringue as you would on a lemon meringue pie—I can't wait to try it soon.

YIELD: 6 servings

SCHOCOLADEN TOPFKUCHEN GERMAN CHRISTMAS EVE CAKE

A wondrous cake adapted by Janet when she was an American Field Student in Germany. It was not used as a Baby Jesus cake there but Janet's family enjoy it on Christmas Eve to celebrate the birth of Baby Jesus.

PREHEAT OVEN to 375 degrees F.

1 cup shortening or 2 cubes margarine	4 jumbo eggs
1-1/2 cups granulated sugar	3 cups flour (cake flour makes lighter cake)
1 teaspoon vanilla or Oetker vanilla sugar	4 teaspoons baking powder
1 lemon (or 2—optional)—juice and rind grated	4 tablespoons cocoa
	2 - 3 tablespoons sugar

Cream shortening or margarine until fluffy and air holes are visible. Add 1-1/2 cups sugar and beat vigorously. Add the grated lemon rind, beating constantly. Size of cake depends on amount of beating. Add eggs one at a time beating after each one. Then add lemon juice and beat. Add flour and baking powder which have been sifted together.

Recipe Continues...

286

SCHOCOLADEN TOPFKUCHEN GERMAN CHRISTMAS EVE CAKE

Continued...

Check batter—if too thick, add a bit of milk. (Batter should not be soupy as with regular cakes.)

Mix cocoa and 3 tablespoons sugar in separate small bowl and add one-third of the cake batter to this.

Spoon one-half of the remaining "white" batter into a greased and well floured Bundt pan or angel food pan. Place chocolate batter on top then add the remaining white batter. Use a knife to slightly marbelize.

Bake at 375 degrees F. for 20 - 25 minutes, then decrease to 350 degrees F. and bake for 30 - 40 minutes. REALLY WATCH OVEN—THIS IS A GERMAN RECIPE AND IT'S TRICKY GUESSING DIFFERENCES IN OVENS. CAKE SHOULD BE GOLDEN BROWN - NOT ANEMIC APPEARING.

Cool on <u>wooden</u> board.

The flavor of the cake is lemon/chocolate.

BONUS: This cake is well worth the effort. It is not at all difficult if you follow step-by-step the instructions. I prefer baking it in a Bundt pan. It is like a pound cake, keeps well and freezes nicely. It is best to make it ahead, and refrigerate air tight—so the flavors can blend.

HOLIDAY CRAN-YAM BETTY-BAKE

This is a fantastic hot dish dessert to serve with the leftover turkey since everyone expects pumpkin pie on Thanksgiving! Don't miss out on this one.

PREHEAT OVEN to 350 degrees F.

1/2 **cup flour**	1/3 **cup butter softened**
1/2 **cup brown sugar**	
1/2 **cup oatmeal**	2 **17 oz. cans yams—sliced**
1 **teaspoon cinnamon**	2 **cups fresh cranberries**

Mix the first five ingredients together. Toss 1 cup of this mixture with the yams and cranberries. Put into 1-1/2 quart buttered casserole and top with the remainder crumbly mixture.

BAKE at 350 degrees F. for 35 minutes.

BONUS: This recipe would double nicely for a larger crowd. It is also a quick dish to make. I think it would be an excellent choice for a holiday brunch.

YIELD: 6-8

WALDORF ASTORIA RED CAKE

This cake was very popular when I was a young bride. It remained so until the "beings who may" decided that the red food coloring was injurious to one's health. Until a new kind of red food coloring was put back on the grocer's shelf, many people tucked away this very famous or "infamous" cake recipe. Anna May is sharing her favored version of "Waldorf Astoria Red Cake."

PREHEAT OVEN: 350 degrees F.

2 8-inch round cake pans
   greased and floured

1-1/2 cups granulated sugar
1/2 cup shortening
2 large eggs
2 tablespoons unsweetened
   cocoa

1 cup low-fat buttermilk
2-1/4 cups CAKE FLOUR
1 teaspoon salt
1 teaspoon baking soda
1/4 cup red food coloring
1 tablespoon vinegar
1 teaspoon vanilla extract

Cream sugar, shortening and eggs. Make paste of cocoa and red food coloring; add to creamed mixture. Add buttermilk alternately with flour and salt which have been stirred together. Mix the soda and vinegar together and blend into batter. Stir in vanilla.

Recipe Continued...

WALDORF ASTORIA RED CAKE
Continued...

Pour half of batter into each cake tin.

BAKE at 350 degrees F. for 25 - 30 minutes.
Remove from oven, cool on racks before frosting.

FROSTING:

3 tablespoons flour
1 cup 2% milk
1 cup butter or margarine

1 cup granulated sugar
1 teaspoon vanilla extract

Cook over medium heat the flour and milk just until thickened.
Remove from heat and cool completely.

With electric mixer, cream the butter and sugar until fluffy.
Add the cooled mixture of flour and milk to the creamed butter and
sugar; add vanilla and continue beating the frosting until texture is
like whipped cream.

Place one layer on cake plate, frost and place second layer on top.
Complete frosting cake.

Recipe Continues...

290

WALDORF ASTORIA RED CAKE
Continued...

BONUS: I sometimes make a 3-layer cake—thus making two complete batches. With the extra layer freeze and use in a trifle dessert.
(See Volume 2 "Best of Friends Too!" for trifle recipe.)

P.S. Cake is perfect for a special Christmas dessert. Also, if someone you know is having a Christmas wedding—this would make a special remembrance for the bride and groom!

P.P.S. Supposedly, the cake was a secret recipe of the Waldorf Astoria Hotel in New York City many moons ago. Ask your mom or grandmom about the story.

❧

AUSTRIAN STRUDEL

Because I mentioned in one of my cookbooks that strudel is hard to make, I was proven to be incorrect in my assumption by a lawyer acquaintance, Francis X. Clinch. The following recipe is a Clinch family recipe and was not only passed on to me to use in this book, but was created by Francis (a young man), and delivered to me, warm from the oven to my place of work. My co-workers and I "legally" adopted this apple strudel. We know you will commence your own adoption proceedings once you have experienced this outstanding traditional favorite.

DOUGH:

2-1/2 cups all purpose flour
1 teaspoon salt
2 eggs slightly beaten

1 tablespoon vegetable oil
2 tablespoons melted butter
1/2 cup warm water

FILLING:

5 cups sliced cooking
   apples
3/4 cup granulated sugar
1/2 cup brown sugar
1 teaspoon cinnamon
   (or to taste)

1/2 teaspoon nutmeg
   (or to taste)
1 cup pecan pieces
6 tablespoons melted butter

Recipe Continues...

AUSTRIAN STRUDEL
Continued...

Combine dough ingredients and knead vigorously for 8 to 10 minutes. Place dough in greased, covered bowl in slightly warm oven for 40 minutes. While dough is resting, prepare filling ingredients, cover your table with cloth and lightly dust cloth with flour.

Remove dough from oven and turn oven to 400 degrees F. Dust dough with flour and knead several times into a ball. Work dough quickly while it is still warm, and work in a warm room free of drafts. Roll dough on cloth into an oblong shape and finish stretching dough by pulling it from below with palms of hands facing down. Dough should be about 30" x 36" and should be very thin.

Cover two-thirds of the dough from short end with the sliced cooking apples. Cover apples with sugar and nuts and dust with spices. Brush uncovered portion of dough with melted butter and drizzle remaining butter over apples. Fold edges of long sides over apples, and roll strudel "jelly-roll" fashion by lifting cloth, starting with end covered with apples. Place strudel on greased cooking sheet, bending to fit and bake in middle of pre-heated oven for 15 minutes. Reduce heat to 325 degrees F. and bake another 45 minutes.

An apple "taffy" will ooze from the strudel during baking, so upon removing from oven, carefully transfer strudel to another cooking sheet. (Kids can eat the taffy after it has cooled slightly).

Serve strudel warm with ice cream, whipped cream or cardamom cream.

Recipe Continued...

AUSTRIAN STRUDEL

Continued...

CARDAMOM CREAM:

3/4 cup whipping cream, well-chilled

1/2 cup brown sugar

1/2 teaspoon ground cardamom

1/2 cup sour cream, well-chilled

Mix whipping cream, brown sugar and cardamom with electric mixer until soft peaks form, blend in the sour cream.

BONUS: The spice cardamom can be found in most grocery stores and specialty kitchen gift stores.

P.S. I use my kitchen table top to roll out the dough. My grandmother used an oil cloth covering; Francis said he uses a white sheet. Whatever works for you is best. Let us know your favorite method.

FLAMING FINALE—
CHERRIES JUBILEE

CHERRIES JUBILEE is awe-inspiring. Kids of all ages love to watch this dessert being created. It can be accomplished quite easily. Take your hands out of the cookie jar and serve this fun dessert for a Christmas eve surprise!

1 1-pound can (2 cups) pitted dark sweet cherries	1/4 cup brandy, kirsch or cherry brandy
1/4 cup granulated sugar	
2 tablespoons cornstarch	Vanilla ice cream

Drain the cherries reserving syrup. In a saucepan, blend the sugar and cornstarch gradually stirring in reserved cherry syrup. Mix well. Over medium heat, cook stirring constantly until mixture thickens and bubbles.

Remove from heat, stir in cherries and pour into a heatproof bowl or into the top pan of a chafing dish, making certain the bottom pan is filled with hot water. Keep hot over flame. Heat brandy or kirsch in a small metal pan with long handle, or if desired, pour heated brandy into a large ladle. Carefully ignite heated brandy and pour over cherry mixture. Stir to blend brandy into the sauce. Serve immediately over ice cream.

BONUS: Turn down the lights before lighting the brandy—this is what gives Cherries Jubilee such a festive touch.

YIELD: 2 cups sauce

CHRISTMAS BIRTHDAY CAKE

A traditional Christmas birthday cake to be served on Christmas Eve. Happy Birthday is sung to Baby Jesus and the cake is then served. A perfect tradition to complement the Christmas Celebration!

One angel food cake—
purchased or home-baked
1 quart vanilla ice cream
1 7 oz. bag "Starlite" round
peppermints
1/2 cup water

2 cups whipping cream
whipped
1/4 cup powdered sugar
1/2 teaspoon vanilla extract

Green Creme de Menthe

Coarsely crush about 40 peppermints in a blender or in a double plastic bag using the side of a hammer.

Whip the cream adding the powdered sugar and vanilla during the process. Store in refrigerator until ready to spread on cake.

In a small saucepan over low heat dissolve 1/2 candies and 1/2 cup water to make a syrup. It will be thin. Slice the cake into 3 layers. Lay the bottom layer on cake plate and drizzle with 2 tablespoons of the syrup and 2 tablespoons crushed candies and 1/2 cup of the whipped cream.

Recipe Continues...

CHRISTMAS BIRTHDAY CAKE

Continued...

The second layer drizzle syrup, crushed candies and whipped cream.

The third layer drizzle syrup, and "frost" the top and sides of cake with remaining whipped cream. Sprinkle some of the crushed mints on sides of cake that has now been frosted with whipped cream.

With a small ice cream scoop, place balls of ice cream in one row around top of cake. Partially freeze the cake at this point to make the crushed candy stick to sides of whipped cream on the cake. Use as much crushed candy as you wish and sprinkle some on top of the ice cream.

Drizzle cake with Creme de Menthe now or after freezing to a firm stage at least one hour or overnight.

BONUS: The cake will take about 30 minutes to asemble. Crushed peppermint sticks can be substituted for the "Starlite" mints if you are unable to find them.

YIELD: Serves 12

❧

297

PAVLOVA

This Australian dessert looks spectacular and tastes spectacular without demanding spectacular effort. Pavlova was a Russian ballerina who performed in Australia in the early 1990's. It is one of my very favorite desserts to prepare and to devour. Please favor your friends and family with this dessert.

4 egg whites
2 teaspoons white vinegar
1/4 teaspoon salt
1 cup granulated sugar
2 cups sliced strawberries,
  kiwi, bananas, peaches,
  papaya or pineapple
  chunks

1 cup whipping cream
1/4 cup granulated sugar
1 teaspoon vanilla

Bring the egg whites to room temperature.
Separate whites from the yolks while the eggs are still cold. It's easier.

Line a baking sheet or 15 x 10 x 1-inch shallow baking pan with brown paper, parchment paper or foil. Using an 8-inch round cake pan as a guide, draw a circle on the paper or foil.

Recipe Continues...

PAVLOVA
Continued...

In a large mixer bowl combine the egg whites, vinegar and salt; beat at medium speed until soft peaks form. Tips will curl.
Gradually add the 1 cup sugar, one tablespoon at a time, beating about 4 minutes more or till mixture forms stiff, glossy peaks (tips will stand straight) and the sugar is dissolved.

Spread about two-thirds of the egg white mixture over the circle to 1/2-inch thickness. Create an edge 1 inch high and 1 inch wide at top of the base.

Spoon remaining mixture into a decorating bag fitted with a large star tip. Pipe mixture in swirls around edge of meringue circle.

For garnish, pipe a small spiral meringue piece for use in the center of finished dessert.

BAKE in a 275 degree F. oven for 1 hour. Turn off heat and let dry in oven with door closed for 2 to 3 hours more. DO NOT OPEN OVEN DOOR WHILE DRYING.

Drain the fruit slices well. Pat the fruit dry with paper towels, if necessary.

Combine whipping cream, the 1/4 cup sugar and vanilla. Beat till soft peaks form.

Recipe Continues...

299

PAVLOVA
Continued...

Carefully remove meringue shell from paper or foil and place on your nicest serving plate. Spoon the whipped cream into meringue shell. Cover with the fruit and meringue spiral if you have made one.

To serve, cut into wedges. Serve immediately. Pass the remaining whipped cream.

BONUS: I make the meringue base early in the morning of the day I plan to serve it. Whip the cream about an hour before dinner and hold it over in the refrigerator. Then complete placement of the fruit, etc. just before calling the guests to the dinner table. It keeps nicely in the refrigerator until you are ready for this truly spectacular dessert.

CALL ME IF YOU HAVE ANY PROBLEMS.

P.S. The recipe is easy to follow step-by-step and I guarantee a perfect result. Read the recipe twice before starting so you become familiar with what you are going to "build."
Other fruits can be substituted if the ones mentioned are not available or are out of season. Raspberries are an excellent substitute for the strawberries.

YIELD: 8 servings

STELLA'S SUPERB FRUITCAKE

Admittedly, I am not much of a fruitcake fan, but Stella's Fruitcake is better than any I have had the pleasure of testing. It also is ideal for "groom's cake" if you have need for one in your future.

2-1/2 cups all purpose flour
1 teaspoon baking soda
2 teaspoons cinnamon
1/2 teaspoon nutmeg
2 large eggs, lightly beaten
1 28-ounce jar mincemeat
1-1/3 cups (1 can) sweetened condensed milk (Eagle Brand)
1-1/2 to 2 cups chopped nuts
8-ounces candied orange peel
8-ounces glazed red cherries - quartered
8-ounces glazed green cherries—quartered
1 to 2 cups golden or regular raisins
Rum or brandy to taste (2 ounces)

Grease 9" tube or spring form pan.
Line with wax paper and grease again.
Sift flour, soda and spices. Combine eggs, mincemeat, condensed milk, nuts, peel, cherries, raisins and rum or brandy. Fold in dry ingredients until well mixed. Pour in pan, add extra nut halves for garnish if desired.

Bake slowly in 300 degree oven for 2 hours until center springs back and the top is golden.

BONUS: This fruit cake improves with age. It also likes the freezer to rest in for a spell. The guarantee is that everyone will enjoy this definitely delectable holiday fruitcake!

MAC'S AMARETTO CHEESECAKE

Actually, this is a "mac"aroon Amaretto cheesecake which recipe comes from my friend "Mac." She came upon this unconventional recipe in one of her searches for a great dessert. Mac made a few excellent additions to the recipe and I know you will want to run to the kitchen soon to perfect one for your next "festive occasion"—which just might be a treat for the office staff on Friday. Go for it!

PREHEAT OVEN: 300 degrees F.
You will need a 9-inch springform pan for baking the cheesecake.

CRUST:

6 medium macaroon cookies
20 vanilla wafer cookies
1/4 cup granulated sugar

4 tablespoons melted butter
1 teaspoon vanilla extract

FILLING:

4 8-ounce packages cream
cheese, softened (low fat
is okay)
1-1/2 cups granulated sugar

4 tablespoons Amaretto
liqueur
1 teaspoon vanilla extract
1 teaspoon almond extract
Pinch of salt
4 eggs

Recipe Continues...

MAC'S AMARETTO CHEESECAKE
Continued...

TOPPING:

2 cups dairy sour cream
   (low fat is okay)
1/4 cup granulated sugar

1 teaspoon almond extract
6 medium macaroons

The macaroons for the crust should be a bit dry. If you happen to get fresh macaroons they will be too soft so "bake" them on a cookie sheet in a 300 degree F. oven about 20 minutes—then let them cool off. Use a food processor or blender to make crumbs with the dried macaroons. You should have at least 2-3/4 cups of crumbs.

Stir in the 1/4 cup sugar, the melted butter and vanilla. The mixture should hold together when pressed; if it doesn't, add a tablespoon or so melted butter. Press the crumb mixture onto the bottom and up the sides of an **ungreased** 9-inch springform pan.

PREHEAT OVEN: 350 degrees F.

Prepare the filling by combining the cream cheese and sugar in the large bowl of an electric mixer, beating at low speed for about 2 to 3 minutes until well mixed. Beat in the Amaretto, vanilla and almond extracts and salt. Add the eggs, one at a time beating with each addition at low speed just until eggs are incorporated. Don't overbeat. Pour the filling into the prepared crust and place on a foil-lined cookie sheet.

Recipe Continued...

MAC'S AMARETTO CHEESECAKE

Continued...

BAKE 45 or 50 minutes for firm bottom and sides—a little gooey in center. If you want it firm throughout, bake for about 60 minutes instead of the 45 or 50 minutes.

Remove baked cheesecake from the oven, leaving the temperature at 350 degrees F. Let the cake set on a rack at room temperature for a **full** 10 minutes while you prepare the topping.

Combine the sour cream, the 1/4 cup of sugar and the almond extract and spread over the slightly cooled cheesecake. Crush the 6 macaroons (listed in the topping ingredients) and sprinkle them over the sour cream topping. **RETURN** cheesecake to the oven and bake another 10 minutes at 350 degrees F. Move the cheesecake directly into the refrigerator and chill it at least 4 hours.

BONUS: The recipe is long but is easy to follow and well worth any extra effort you may expend. How about serving this with a New Year's Day brunch. What a way to start a NEW YEAR!

Mac also suggests that a little less than 2 cups of sour cream is better for the topping mix. I used about 1-3/4 cups.

YIELD: 12 to 16 servings

CHOCOLATE &
FRESH RASPBERRIES

This absolutely overwhelming chocolate dessert is just the perfect Valentine Day Dessert to present to your very favorite Valentine!!**! The recipient will love you forever.

2 cups all purpose flour
2 cups granulated sugar
2 teaspoons ground
  cinnamon
1 cup butter or margarine
4 tablespoons unsweetened
  cocoa

1 cup water
1/2 cup buttermilk or sour
  cream
2 eggs
1 teaspoon baking soda
2 teaspoons vanilla

FROSTING:

1/2 cup butter or margarine
4 tablespoons unsweetened
  cocoa

4 tablespoons low fat milk
4 cups confectioner's sugar
1/2 teaspoon vanilla

RASPBERRY FILLING:

4 tablespoons premium
  quality raspberry
  preserves

2 cups fresh raspberries
(whole frozen ones can be
used)

PREHEAT OVEN: 350 degrees F.

Recipe Continues...

305

CHOCOLATE & FRESH RASPBERRIES
Continued...

In a large bowl, mix the flour, sugar and cinnamon.
In a small sauce pan combine butter, water and cocoa, bringing to a boil. Pour chocolate mixture over flour and sugar. Mix well. Mix buttermilk, eggs, soda and vanilla together and beat until smooth. Add to chocolate mixture and beat until smooth.

Pour into 9" x 13" pan which has been greased and dusted with flour.

BAKE for 35 to 45 minutes or until toothpick comes out of center clean. **DO NOT OVERBAKE.** Remove pan from oven and place on a wire rack.

While cake is baking, melt butter and coca for frosting. Stir in milk. Do not boil. Remove from heat and add the confectioner's sugar, mix well and blend in vanilla.

Spread raspberry preserves over warm cake. Place fresh whole raspberries on top of the preserves and flatten just slightly with a fork. Spoon frosting over raspberries and spread carefully with a knife. Cake should be frosted while warm.

BONUS: This cake is delicious warm or cold. I found the frosting to be too thick to spread. I added a little leftover coffee from breakfast to the frosting to thin it—great idea.
Also, I used a chocolate cake mix to speed up the process and it works just fine if you're in a bind for time.

Recipe Continued...

CHOCOLATE & FRESH RASPBERRIES
Continued...

I use seedless raspberry jelly and use a pastry brush to apply the jelly on the warm cake. I also use more than the 4 tablespoons alotted in the recipe.

Cake is best eaten the day of baking. Doesn't it just make your mouth water reading this recipe. DON'T WAIT UNTIL VALENTINE'S DAY TO BAKE ONE. Serve with vanilla or coffee flavored ice cream on top.

YIELD: 16 servings

MINCEMEAT/PUMPKIN TARTS

For those of us who need just a "touch of sweet" after a lavish Thanksgiving feast, these magnificent little tarts are just what the doctor ordered!

Refrigerated ready-made pie crust

PREHEAT OVEN: 375 degrees F.

Prepare pie crust as directions dictate for a single crust pie.

Roll out thinly to slightly less than 1/8 inch.
Using a fluted cookie or pastry cutter, cut out twelve 4-inch circles.
Press lightly into ungreased 2-3/4-inch muffin tins. DO NOT PRICK THE PASTRY.

FILLING:

1 cup canned pumpkin
1/3 cup granulated sugar
1/2 teaspoon pumpkin pie
   spice

1/2 cup low fat milk
1/2 cup prepared mincemeat
Sweetened whipped cream
Pecan halves

In a medium mixing bowl combine egg, pumpkin, sugar and pumpkin pie spice. Mix well. Stir in the milk. Place about 1 teaspoon of the mincemeat mix in each tart shell; top with about 2 tablespoons of the pumpkin pie mixture.

Recipe Continues...

MINCEMEAT/PUMPKIN TARTS
Continued...

BAKE pumpkin tarts in 375 degree F. oven for 25 to 30 minutes or until a knife inserted off-center comes out clean.

Cool tarts on wire rack. Cover and store in refrigerator.
Just before serving garnish with the sweetened whipped cream and a pecan half.

BONUS: If you don't have pumpkin pie spice, mix your own with cinnamon, nutmeg, cloves, etc. from your cupboard. Also, be sure to flavor your sweetened whipped cream with a little vanilla.

I like to use my mini-muffin tin to make these tarts. Simply use a smaller cookie or biscuit cutter to cut the pie crust and cut down on the amount of filling. I have been successful in freezing the baked tarts. When cleaning out my freezer this summer, I found a small cache of the tarts which were thoroughly enjoyed by me and my "best friends."

YIELD: 12 tarts

MINTED MACAROONS

The best macaroons I've had the pleasure to test and taste. Great holiday cookie plate fillers.

PREHEAT OVEN: 300 degrees F.

Lightly grease cookie sheet.

3 large egg whites
1/4 teaspoon cream of tartar
1/8 teaspoon salt

3/4 cup granulated sugar
1/4 teaspoon peppermint
   extract
2 cups flaked coconut
3/4 cup miniature pastel-
   colored mint candy kisses

Beat egg whites, cream of tartar and salt in small mixer bowl until just foamy. Beat in the sugar 1 tablespoon at a time; continue beating until stiff and glossy. DO NOT UNDERBEAT. Pour into medium bowl. Fold in peppermint extract, coconut and candy kisses.

Drop the mixture by teaspoonfuls onto cookie sheet, about 1 inch apart. Place a candy mint on each cookie. Bake 20 to 25 minutes or just until edges start to turn light brown.

Remove cookies from oven, cool 10 minutes before removing from cookie sheet.

BONUS: If desired, you can use 3/4 cup miniature milk chocolate or semisweet chocolate chips to replace the mint candy kisses.

YIELD: 32 - 36 cookies

KRUM KAKKE

Krum Kakke is a special holiday treat. This recipe comes from my friend's family album. It is traditional and the entire family is included in the festivity.

You will need a Krum Kakke iron which can be purchased in most kitchen and cookware stores.

Preheat Krum Kakke iron

2 cups granulated sugar
1 cup melted butter

4 eggs well beaten
1 cup milk

1 teaspoon baking powder
3 cups all purpose flour
1 teaspoon vanilla extract

In a large mixing bowl cream together the sugar and butter. Add the beaten eggs, milk, baking powder, flour and vanilla.

Pour teaspoonful on griddle, turn over in 30 - 60 seconds to brown the other side. Remove with spatula and roll up with Krum Kakke wooden rod immediately.

BONUS: Joyce says this recipe makes a large amount so she usually makes just half of the recipe.

ROSETTES

Unbelievable "non-stick" rosette batter. The secret to this recipe is the water. Try them now—don't wait for Christmas!

1/2 cup all purpose flour
1 tablespoon granulated
  sugar
1/2 cup cold water

1 large egg
1 tablespoon melted butter
  or margarine

Mix the flour and sugar together; add the water, egg and melted butter. Proceed as you would for making rosettes.

BONUS: Be sure to dip the rosette iron into the hot oil before dipping the iron into the batter.

YIELD: Depends on size of rosette iron. Batter can be doubled.

SUGAR CUT-OUTS

These yummy sugar cookies are incredibly easy to create. The dough can be rolled very thin without "tearing" the shape you wish to cut out. Fill that cookie jar to the brim soon!

PREHEAT OVEN: 350 degrees F.

1 cup butter (don't use
   margarine)
1 cup granulated sugar
1 egg slightly beaten
1/4 cup sour cream
3 cups all purpose flour

1/2 teaspoon nutmeg—freshly
   grated is best
1 teaspoon soda
1/4 teaspoon salt
2 teaspoons vanilla

Use mixer to blend butter until very creamy. Mix in sugar gradually. Add egg and sour cream, mix well. Add all dry ingredients which have been stirred together. Chill the dough for 1 hour.

Lightly grease cookie sheet.

Divide dough into three pieces. On a lightly floured bread board roll out one piece of dough at a time. Using your favorite cookie cutters, proceed. Keep creating until all dough is used. You can use the scraps of dough by gathering into a ball and rolling it out on board.

Recipe Continues:

SUGAR CUT-OUTS
Continued...

Place cut-outs on greased cookie sheet. Bake at 350 degrees F. for 8 to 10 minutes. Cool slightly before removing cookies from cookie sheet onto racks.

BONUS: You can sprinkle colored sugars on pre-baked cookies or frost to decorate after cookies have baked and cooled—be ingenious. These cookies freeze nicely—if they are not immediately gobbled in record time.

YIELD: 24 - 36

VICTORIA TEA PASTRY

An effortless holiday treat for those early morning hours or late afternoon after-shopping "tea and crumpet" breaks.

PREHEAT OVEN: 350 degrees F.

1 cup water
1/2 cup margarine DO NOT
   USE BUTTER
2 cups all purpose flour
1/2 cup margarine—softened

2 tablespoons water
3 eggs
1 teaspoon almond extract
   flavoring

In a medium size saucepan, bring 1 cup water and 1/2 cup margarine to a boil. Remove from heat and stir in one cup flour with a wooden spoon. Beat until smooth.

In a small bowl, combine one cup flour and 1/2 cup margarine. Blend well, add 2 tablespoons water and mix until ball forms. Divide the ball in half and place on an ungreased cookie sheet. Flatten into two 1/4 inch thick strips, each measuring 2" x 12". Keep the strips one inch apart on the cookie sheet.

Add the three eggs one at a time to the mix in the saucepan, beating after each addition. Again, use a wooden spoon. Stir in vanilla and almond flavoring.

Spread the latter mixture on each strip of dough to within 1/2 inch of the edges.

Recipe Continues...

315

VICTORIA TEA PASTRY

Continued...

Bake 1 hour at 350 degrees F. without opening the oven.

Remove from oven, cool 10 minutes and frost.

FROSTING:

1/4 cup butter softened
1 cup powdered sugar
1 tablespoon milk

1/2 teaspoon almond extract

1/4 to 1/2 cup sliced almonds
   toasted

Place almonds on a cookie sheet and watching carefully toast them about 2 - 3 minutes. Watch very carefully so the almonds do not burn.

Combine the butter, sugar, milk and almond extract. Spread over warm pastries. Sprinkle with the toasted nuts.

Slice pastry and serve with the appropriate beverage depending on what time of day it is.

BONUS: The pastry can be frozen, but best taste and texture comes fresh from the oven.

AMARETTI COOKIES

Undiluted and simple, these absolutely habit-forming cookies have an ingredient unavailable to the vast majority. I have found a substitute for "bitter almonds" which is a necessary ingredient that definitely fashions the "unusual taste" of Amaretti.

1 cup bitter almonds ground—I substitute apricot stones which are available at health food stores.

3 cups sweet almonds ground—just plain almonds

2 cups granulated sugar
2 cups powdered sugar
1 teaspoon baking powder

7 egg whites, lightly beaten
1 teaspoon almond extract

Beat the egg whites slightly and stir in the almond extract.

To the egg white and extract mixture, add the almond and sugar combination. Cover with plastic wrap and leave on counter overnight or 12 hours.

Line cookie sheets with parchment paper and drop small rounded teaspoonfuls on lined cookie sheets. Space at least about 2 inches apart as the dough spreads out as it bakes.

Recipe Continues...

AMARETTI COOKIES
Continued...

The recipe given to me says that waxed paper is a good substitute for parchment paper. It didn't work for me. Brown paper would probably be a better substitute if you don't have parchment paper.

BAKE at 325 degrees F. for 12 minutes.
Watch carefully as it is possible to overbake.

Let cool on paper 7 to 10 minutes before removing to avoid breaking.

If using a heavy aluminum pan, add 3 minutes to the baking time.

BONUS: I must reiterate that these cookies are absolutely habit forming. Keep them in a "locked" cookie tin and throw away the key if you don't want to become addicted. The apricot stones I bought at the health food store have a note on the package that says "Could have toxic reaction". I have not had any reaction and my aunt Esther says she and her childhood friends used to eat the apricot pits even though they were bitter—no one told them they were harmful.

YIELD: 7 - 8 dozen depending on size

SWEET SHOPPE:

SWEET SHOPPE
Index

CHOCOLATE PEANUT BUTTER FINGERS

These scrumptious peanut butter and chocolate butter fingers are my favorite to eat and to make. A very special addition to any Christmas basket or the ideal house gift during the holidays.

2 cups confectioner's sugar
1 12-ounce jar crunchy
  peanut butter

1 cup raisins (optional)
4 tablespoons melted butter

Mix all of the above ingredients together by hand. Shape in small balls or finger shaped logs. The cookies are very rich so do not make large.

Chill the balls or fingers before dipping in their "chocolate bath."

CHOCOLATE BATH:

1 12-ounce package
  chocolate chips

1/2 bar paraffin

Recipe Continues...

CHOCOLATE PEANUT BUTTER FINGERS
Continued...

Melt the chocolate chips and paraffin in a double boiler.
Use a toothpick or bamboo skewer to dip each ball into the Chocolate Bath. Place on wax paper lined cookie sheet. Cover the hole made in the cookie by pouring a bit of melted chocolate decoratively over it. Cool and refrigerate.

BONUS: Store in refrigerator or cookies can be frozen.
Your family will "flip" over these delectable peanut butter/chocolate treats.

DARLENE'S RUM BALLS

This recipe goes back many years when I first went to work for the law office where I still hang out. My friend Lee and two of our mutual friends made these delectable Christmas cookies every year. I misplaced my recipe but retrieved it from Lee who still thinks these Rum Balls are the greatest...so do I!

1/2 **pound Vanilla Wafers,**
  finely ground
1 **cup finely ground walnuts**
  or pecans
1 **cup confectioners sugar**

2 **tablespoons chocolate,**
  melted
1/2 **cup corn syrup**
1/4 **cup light rum**

Combine all ingredients in a large bowl. Mix very well. The mixture should be stiff and smooth. Roll into small balls... 2 inches in diameter or smaller if you prefer. Roll in confectioners sugar. Set in a dry cool place about 24 hours before serving.

YIELD: 2-1/2 - 3 dozen

BONUS: Store these cookies in an air tight container. The flavor improves with age.

❧

323

B'S MAGNIFICENT FUDGE

Long known as the best fudge in town, my mother-in-law without fail made what seemed to me to be "tons" of it every Christmas. Certainly a tradition, she shared her fudge with many people and they still remember it. Amazing as it may seem, no one in our family had the recipe. A friend of mine who loved B's fudge had gotten the recipe many, many years ago and I finally retrieved it from her. It is extremely easy and fail-proof. I know you will enjoy it all year long.

4-1/2 cups granulated sugar
1 12 oz. can evaporated milk
1 cup butter

1 7 oz. jar marshmallow creme

2 12 oz. packages chocolate morsels

2 cups walnuts—in big pieces

NO VANILLA

Bring the first three ingredients to boil while stirring. Boil for 6 minutes, remove from heat and pour over remaining ingredients which have been placed in large saucepan. Add walnuts if desired and stir until just blended. Spoon fudge into two well-buttered 9" x 13" pans—spread to all edges. Let fudge set up at room temperature, then you may want to keep it refrigerated.

Recipe Continues...

B'S MAGNIFICENT FUDGE
Continued...

BONUS: I sometimes use heart-shaped plastic molds such as the Hallmark cookie holders available during Valentine's Day, or plastic molds for Christmas, etc. Any other kind of mold will work as long as it is buttered very well.

P.S. B's Fudge freezes very well. I don't know why she said not to use vanilla, but I don't and the fudge is wonderful—and addictive.

YIELD: 4-1/2 to 5 pounds

ANGEL FLAKE CHOCOLATES

Also known as Lady Baltimore candy to some. An extraordinary treat to add to your Christmas candy and cookie trays. Also a candy that doesn't necessitate cooking so you can prepare on a rainy or snowy day.

1/2 pound sweet butter
1 2-pound bag of confectioners sugar
1 can sweetened condensed milk such as Borden's Eagle Brand
2 cups Angel Flake coconut

2/3 cup finely chopped pecans

1 12-ounce package milk chocolate morsels (chocolate chips)
1/4 pound paraffin

Mix together all of the ingredients except the chocolate chips and paraffin. Chill mixture about two hours.

Melt the chocolate chips and paraffin in a double boiler.

Using about 1 teaspoon of the fondant (first mixture), roll into balls and store in refrigerator until ready to dip in melted chocolate/paraffin.

Recipe Continues...

ANGEL FLAKE CHOCOLATES
Continued...

Using a toothpick or a 6 to 8 inch bamboo stick, dip the balls into the chocolate and dry on waxed paper. After all balls have been dipped, dip stick or small spoon into the chocolate and let a drop fall over the hole left in the candy when removing the toothpick after dipping.

BONUS: I have used fresh huckleberries and placed two of them on a half piece of the fondant ball and then covering the berries with the other half piece of the fondant ball enclosing the huckleberries completely; then dip in chocolate and complete the drying process.

P.S. Store in air tight container and keep refrigerated.

FUDGE BY THE SPOONFUL

Anna May created this drop fudge from her regular "cut-by-the-square" recipe. It is an innovative technique and packages nicely for a gift.

2 cups granulated sugar
2 squares unsweetened
  chocolate
1/3 cup corn syrup—such as
  Karo brand
1/2 cup 2% milk
Dash of salt

1/2 teaspoon vanilla
3/4 of 1/4 pound of butter
  (6 ounces)
1/2 cup chopped nuts
  (if desired)

In a large saucepan dump the first five (5) ingredients and cook until mixture reaches a soft ball stage (235 to 238 degrees F. on a candy thermometer or when using the "cold water" test—drop a bit of the hot mixture into a small bowl of cold water.)

Remove from heat and add the butter. Cool mixture 30 to 60 minutes. Add 1/2 teaspoon vanilla and beat in the same saucepan until thick. Add chopped walnuts if desired.

Drop thickened fudge by teaspoon onto wax paper.

BONUS: If fudge doesn't "behave" well enough to drop, pour into a buttered pan and cut into squares.

YIELD: Depends on size of "drops"

❧

TRIPLE TREAT CLUSTERS

You can make up your own "triple treat" chocolate clusters but the combination below is my favorite!

1 12-ounce package semisweet chocolate morsels
1 12-ounce package milk chocolate morsels

2 pounds white chocolate (candy discs or white chocolate morsels)
1 24-ounce jar unsalted dry-roasted peanuts.

Melt chocolate in electric skillet on low setting or in a double boiler. Stir constantly during the melting process. Remove from heat and cool 5 minutes. Stir in peanuts and drop mixture by tablespoonfuls onto waxed paper. Cool completely. Wrap individually in plastic wrap. Store in refrigerator until ready to serve.

BONUS: I buy my "white" chocolate from our local candy maker but white chocolate discs can be found at most candy and cake decorating stores. These clusters are really delicious and extraordinarily simple to create.

YIELD: 66 to 72 pieces depending how large you make the clusters

BLUE RIBBON PEANUT BRITTLE

Indubitably the best! Easily created in a microwave—no one will believe it.

1-1/2 cups unsalted dry-roasted peanuts (7 to 8 ounces)
1 cup granulated sugar
1/2 cup light corn syrup

1/8 teaspoon salt
1 tablespoon butter
1 teaspoon vanilla extract
1-1/4 teaspoons baking soda

Butter a large cookie sheet. In large microwave bowl, combine peanuts, sugar, corn syrup and salt. Microwave on High until mixture bubbles vigorously—approximately 6 minutes. Remove from microwave and stir in butter and vanilla. Return bowl to microwave and cook on High until candy turns light golden, about 3 minutes. Remove from microwave. Quickly add the baking soda to candy, stirring briskly. Mixture will foam up.

Immediately pour brittle out onto a prepared baking sheet. Shake baking sheet from side to side spreading mixture as thinly as possible. Let cool and harden. This should take about 2 hours. Break into desired size pieces.

BONUS: Best stored in airtight container at room temperature. Will keep for a month. Also can be frozen.

P.S. Cooking time of microwave may vary because of differences in power.

YIELD: Approximately 1 pound

PRALINES,
NEW ORLEANS STYLE

Pralines are indulgent IF you choose suitable weather to pursue this task. A dry day is the key to developing a nice supply of these tasteful candies. Don't pass up your chance to surprise your family and friends with a nice cache of pralines.

2 cups granulated sugar	1/2 cup evaporated milk
1 cup firmly packed golden brown sugar	2 tablespoons unsalted butter
1/2 cup whipping cream (old style)	1/4 teaspoon salt
	3 cups pecans

Line 2 large baking sheets with wax paper.
Combine all ingredients, except the pecans, in a large heavy saucepan. Stir over medium heat until mixture boils. Add pecans and cook until candy thermometer registers 234 degrees F., stirring frequently. This should take about 10 minutes. Remove mixture from heat, stir slowly for 10 SECONDS ONLY.

Work with speed, dropping mixture generously by spoonfuls onto prepared baking sheets.

Recipe Continues...

PRALINES, NEW ORLEANS STYLE

Continued...

Let pralines stand until set—at least 2 hours. Peel pralines off paper and store in airtight container at room temperature.

BONUS: If you do not heed my warning and decide to make pralines on a humid day, set up an electric fan to blow on the pralines enabling them to set up accurately.

P.S. It is important to work quickly in forming the pralines as the candy stiffens in the pan in a wink of an eye.

YIELD: 24 - 30

❦

GARNET'S EXCLUSIVE MINTS

Exclusive to "Best of Friends'" followers, these mints are easy to create especially when a friend joins in the festivities. It brings back memories of the "taffy pulling" parties of years gone by. These yummy candies will undoubtedly become a holiday tradition at your house, too.

2 cups granulated sugar	1 cup water
1/4 pound (1 stick) butter	

Heat butter and water together until butter is melted. Add sugar and stir only until sugar is dissolved. Cook on high to 220 degrees F. on a candy thermometer. Turn heat to low and cook to 258 degrees F. Pour onto a marble slab or cookie sheet that has been chilled. Dot with food coloring if desired.

When mixture has hardened around the edges, grease hands with butter. Rub oil of peppermint on your hands and "pull" candy like you would pull taffy until it loses its gloss. (It will look dry rather than "wet.") This should take about 10 minutes.
This is the time a good friend is helpful.

Pull into a narrow rope and cut with scissors into bite size pieces. Store in a tightly covered can until mints "mellow." They will be hard but will soften in the can in two to three days.

BONUS: These candies are good travelers if you are mailing goodies during the holidays. Also, be sure to pack them in your suitcase so they won't get "nibbled away" before you get to your destination.

CARMEN'S BUTTER CRUNCH

My mouth is watering as I write this recipe. Indisputably the best pecan crunch I have ever had the privilege of testing and eating. I can guarantee not a "speck" will be left on the serving tray, but if there is, it is friendly to the freezer.

1 cup chopped pecans
1/2 cup granulated sugar
1/2 cup butter (don't
   substitute)

1 tablespoon light corn
   syrup

Line the bottom of a 9-inch pie pan with aluminum foil—butter the foil and set aside. (Do not use wax paper or plastic wrap.)

Combine pecans, sugar, butter and corn syrup in a 10-inch heavy skillet. Over medium heat, bring the mixture to a boil, stirring constantly with a wooden spoon. Continue boiling and stirring the mixture until candy turns golden brown or about 6 to 10 minutes.

Working quickly, spread the crunch in the prepared pie pan. Cool 5 minutes or until firm. Remove from pan by lifting edges of foil—peeling off the foil.

Candy may be presented as a disk or broken into pieces and stored in a jar.

BONUS: The butter crunch is great fun and delicious too! I'm heading to the kitchen to make a batch right now. ENJOY!

YIELD: 3/4 pound

❧

DIVINE DIVINITY

*Most of us have not had good luck making divinity divine.
Connie's mother knows the trick! Read on.....*

3 cups granulated sugar	3 egg whites, stiffly beaten
2/3 cup golden Karo syrup	Nuts, cherries or coconut
2/3 cup cold water	(see below)

In a large saucepan stir the first three ingredients to a boil; then boil
to a hard thread (250 degrees F. or 126 - 130 degrees C). Slowly
pour the hot mixture into three stiffly beaten egg whites. Beat well
and add 1-1/2 teaspoons vanilla. Add 1/2 cup nuts or 1/2 cup
maraschino cherries (well drained and chopped) or 1 cup moist pack
coconut.

After beating and beating if candy does not set up, place bowl in a
pan of hot water. It will set up quickly as you continue to beat—even
on a damp, rainy day.

You can drop by teaspoon onto wax paper or pour into a buttered
Pyrex dish and cut in squares.

BONUS: I use my hand mixer to beat the divinity. Also I add a little
red or green food coloring to make pink and green divinity for
Christmas.

P.S. Also—I do not choose to make any of my candies on a rainy
or wintry day.

JR. MINTS BY JO-JO

Remember those great little chocolate covered mints of the 50's? Well, here's your chance to re-kindle that memory and taste.
Jo-Jo is sharing her "Junior Mints" with us and they are better than ever.

3 tablespoons sweet butter—
   softened
3 tablespoons corn syrup

1/2 teaspoon peppermint
   extract
2-1/2 cups powdered sugar

Mix together all of the above ingredients until smooth. If mixture is sticky, add more powdered sugar. Roll into small balls, flatten in palms of your hands 3/4 inch or smaller than a quarter. Place on wax paper-lined cookie sheet. Freeze one-half hour or longer. Jo-Jo splits a batch on two cookie sheets.

CHOCOLATE COVERING:

1 11-1/2 oz. package of
   mint-flavored chocolate
   chips

1/4 bar paraffin wax (break
   in small pieces for
   quicker melting)

Recipe Continues...

JR. MINTS BY JO-JO
Continued...

Melt the chocolate and paraffin wax in double boiler. Poke a mint with toothpick and dip in chocolate. If it drops off, freeze mints until harder. Let extra chocolate drip off, then twist toothpick to loosen mint. Place back on cookie sheet. If mints soften while dipping, refreeze. Cover the hole left by toothpick with your initial using a toothpick dipped in chocolate. Refrigerate until ready to serve.

BONUS: I keep an old saucepan for melting chocolate and paraffin. DO NOT ATTEMPT TO MELT WAX DIRECTLY OVER BURNER –USE ONLY THE DOUBLE BOILER METHOD. The wax and chocolate are a bit difficult to clean up and you don't want your sink to get clogged with the wax. There are other recipes using the melted wax and chocolate method—so hunt for a used saucepan at the weekly rummage sales or flea markets in your area. You can save any leftover chocolate in a jar in your refrigerator for the next session. Just melt in jar and add to a new batch in the saucepan. (I place my old, smaller saucepan into a larger pan to "make" a double boiler.)

P.S. After you have made your first batch of chocolate dipped candy, you will hunt out more things to use the chocolate/wax method.

YIELD: 50 to 60 mints

337

CHRISTMAS PEPPERMINT CREME CRUNCH

A no-fail spectacular confection that can be formulated even on the snowiest of days. I can hardly wait for the "season" so I can make this peppermint creme crunch.

2 pounds white chocolate

1/2 **pound red and green peppermint candy canes— crushed into small pieces**

Melt white chocolate over medium heat stirring until smooth. I use my electric fry pan. Remove from heat and stir in the crushed peppermint sticks.

Pour on wax paper lined cookie sheets and spread the candy towards the edges of the cookie sheet.

Chill in refrigerator—about 10 minutes. Break into various size pieces—as for peanut brittle or toffee. Store in air tight containers.

BONUS: I use vanilla "wafers" which can be purchased at a candy making supply house or sometimes your local chocolatier will sell you a supply of white chocolate if you give him ample notice. I don't think "almond bark" will do the recipe justice.

Purchase the peppermint sticks at any local supermarket during the holiday season and stock up after Christmas when the candy canes go on sale. Just pop them in your freezer for the next year.

YIELD: 2-1/2 pounds

FLAVORED POPCORN BALLS

A colorful, yummy and especially easy method of creating festive popcorn balls. Kids of all ages will certainly have fun with this recipe.

2 cups corn syrup—such as
    Karo brand
2 cups granulated sugar

1 6-ounce package gelatin—
    any flavor
——
4 - 5 quarts popped
    popcorn

Mix first three ingredients together in a saucepan and bring to a boil. Remove from heat and pour over popcorn. Butter hands, let popcorn cool a little, form into balls.

BONUS: Use red and green-colored gelatins for a Christmas theme. My favorite red is Raspberry. Wrap in colored plastic for storage and gift giving.

GENERAL INDEX

GENERAL INDEX
(Continued)

342

GENERAL INDEX
(Continued)

GENERAL INDEX
(Continued)